D1592058

FIELD NOTES.

THE ZOOLOGICAL TIMES TABLE

And Spotters' Identification Guide

Vertical Column :
1. Hawk.
2. Wild Narwhal.
3. Tortoise.
4. Giraffe.
5. Piranha.

A. Moose.
B. Mean Squid.
C. Ape.
D. Locust OR Grasshopper.
E. Housecat.

A1. Moosehawk.
B1. Squawk. (doubles as call)
C1. Hape.
D1. Hawkhopper.
E1. Hawkat.

A2. Moosewhal.
B2. Squidwhal.
C2. Narwhape.
D2. Narwhopper.
E2. Catwhal.

A3. Moortoise.
B3. Shelled Squid.
C3. Tortape.
D3. Tortust.
E3. Armadillo.

A4. Girmoose.
B4. Squiraffid.
C4. Aperaffe.
D4. Girocust.
E4. Something from a Miyazaki film..

A5. Piranhamoose.
B5. Piranhasquid.
C5. Piranhape.
D5. Piranhahopper.
E5. The saddest thing

Grateful acknowledgement is made for permission to reprint this chart from the Journal of the Institute for Absurd Ideas, Volume CXVII, No. 14.

F. Rhinoceros.
G. Walrus.
H. Eagle.
I. Common Horse.
J. Bull Elephant.

F6. Squidoceros.
G6. Walrusquid.
H6. Squeagle.
I6. Squorse.
J6. Squelephant.

F7. Rhinwhal.
G7. Walrwhal.
H7. Narwheagle.
I7. Real Unicorn.
J7. Narwhelephant.

F8. Rhimel.
G8. Camwhal.
H8. Cameagel.
I8. Hormel.
J8. Camelephant.

F9. Rhinbat.
G9. Batrus.
H9. Beagel.
I9. Horbat.
J9. Batlephant.

F10. Rhinmingo.
G10. Flahrus.
H10. Flameagle.
I10. Flamequus.
J10. The best thing I've ever seen, bar none, and I've seen Mount Rushmore

Emperor of the Food Chain,

OR

A THRILLING CATALOGUE

OF

NEW, PROPOSED, AND SUGGESTED

ANIMALS,

RECOMMENDED FOR IMMEDIATE DEVELOPMENT BY

Mad Scientists, Alchemists, and Irregular Zoologists

—AS WELL AS A BUNCH OF COMIC STRIPS AND OTHER NONSENSE.

BY

DAVID MALKI !, P.P.-A.S.E.L.

ASSISTANT COMMISSARY GENERAL TO H.M. FORCES. CORRESPONDING MEMBER OF THE NATURAL HISTORY SOCIETY OF VENICE; HONORARY MEMBER OF THE HISTORIC SOCIETY OF AMBULATORY BEASTS IN PRAGUE; MEMBER OF THE SOCIETY OF POMPOSITY AND SELF-RIDICULE, &C. &. &C.

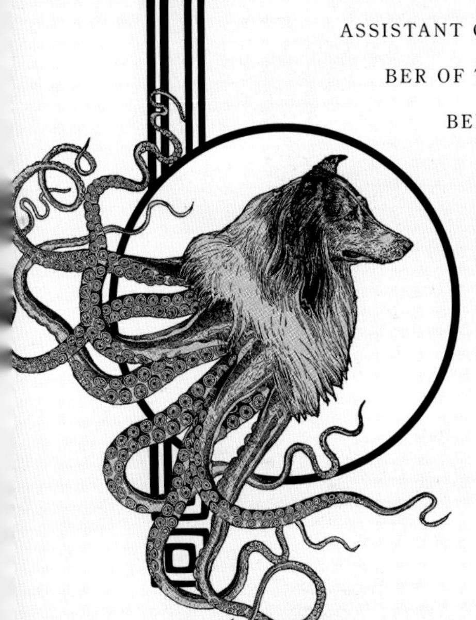

Easthampton:

PUBLISHED BY TOPATOCO BOOKS,

PLEASANT ST.

MMXII.

WONDERMARK ❖ AN ILLUSTRATED JOCULARITY.

The Title of Record of this Volume is : Wondermark: Emperor of the Food Chain.™

FIRST PRINTING— SEPTEMBER 2012— FOR YOUR ENJOYMENT.

Additional Content By

Pages 11, 15, 19, 23, 27, 31, 25, 39, 43, 47, 51, 55, 59, 63, 67, 71, 78 : Color ~ **Anthony Clark**
Pages 89–100, 112 : Color ~ **Marcus "Parcus" Thiele**
Pages 101-104 : Artwork ~ **Phil McAndrew** / Story ~ **Sharon Bryan**

ISBN-13: 978-1-936561-93-3

PUBLISHED BY TOPATOCO BOOKS ; *A division of The Topato Corporation*
116 Pleasant St., Ste 203—Easthampton, MA 01027
topatoco.com / wondermark.com

PRINTED IN CHINA

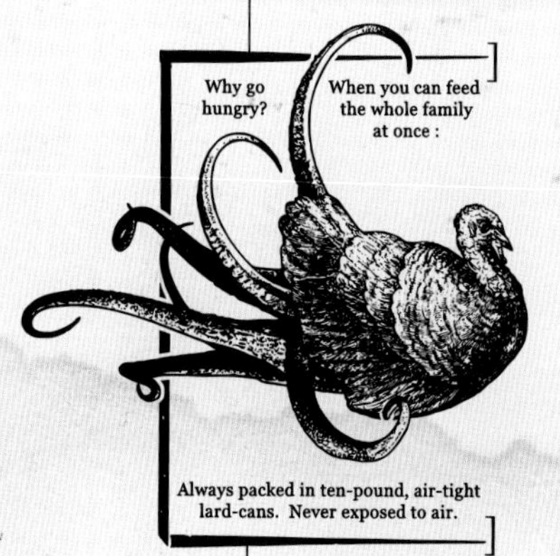

ENJOY "TURCTOPUS."

The Meal That Guarantees "Everyone Gets A Drumstick!"

ENGINEERED AND PROCESSED BY

PILGRIM'S INK,

MONTREAL AND BOSTON.

TABLE OF CONTENTS

For This Very Volume.

WM
WONDERMARK

We Will Eat Any animal you like, at any time you please. No insect too disgusting, no foal or puppy too young and tender. Have an infestation of any sort? We are famished for it. Write at once to Chief Protein Ingestor, Desk 50, *The Bro-On-A-Bet Company, 381 Fourth Ave., N.Y.City.*

Write Like A Smart Owl

Would you like to have penmanship as marvelous as the wisest owl in the forest? Now you can have the equivalent of PERSONAL INSTRUCTION from one of the *craggiest old owls ever* with our handy *study-at-home* BOOKLET AND LESSON SERIES.

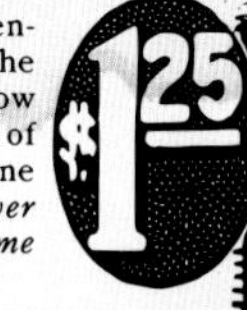

ONLY THE BEST OWLS. We went into the darkest forest and paid the oldest owl we could find to write a bunch of stuff for us with his scratchy talon. Then we reverse-engineered it, in order to teach you how to write just the same. Order with confidence: *This owl was straight-up wearing a mortarboard.* OWL-PRO Co, De't "O," New Orleans.

ARMADILLOS

are soft, easeful, soothing

Wear them in the house instead of stiff leather shoes. Styles for every member of the family.

Daniel Armadillo Shoe Co.
105 East 13th St., New York

"Arm and Dillo," a wonderful story book for children, sent on request.

For Pets & Livestock

The addition of Human Blood and Organ Meat to feed automatically damns animals to an afterlife of hellfire.

Punish misbehaving animals in the hereafter without them even realizing what you're doing. Additive packets provided by post.

Sample and literature free. Brooks Curse Co. Boston, Mass.

BROOKS' HumanFLESH
For the animal you want to BURN

WANT TO BE A HORSE?

2 year course. Send stamp for Catalog.
THE IMAGINATION CORRAL OF PHILADELPHIA
Cor. 23rd and Chestnut Sts. Philadelphia

Send Us Your

Dead Pets

Furry, Scaly, Or Any Other

We tan their deceased hide by our special process of cleaning, combing, carding, and respinning. Then we dye it and weave new

Velvety Rugs

in plain, fancy or Oriental patterns—*any color you want, any size*—the equal of the high-priced store rugs.

You Save $10 to $30

and get beautiful, reversible, *seamless*, soft, bright, *new* rugs, made of your precious friends. We pay you for your material if not satisfied. Every order guaranteed of *mild* scent.

FREE Write for our list of techinques for hastening grumpy pets' path to the rug-centric party future.

ANIMAL ORGAN HARVESTERS.
Dept. D-31,36 Laflin St.,Chicago, Ill

ELEPHANTS

Discount Surplus

We have extra elephants left over from hard labor that we are willing to clear out at prices never before offered to the public or even to any of our wholesalers.

4 Types To Choose From

Gray ones, pinkish ones, ones that wheeze, even a few with spirit left in the eye, all larger than any man.

Five Of These Beasts Postpaid for 25c.

Along with our unique recipe book with barbecue sauces, just in case you decide to go that way.

E. LIQUIDATORS., Dept. H, Cleveland, Oh.

Tennant's "Non-Insect" SOAP

NO MORE CARAPACE FRAGMENTS IN BATH.

ARE YOU STILL USING insect-based soap? TENNANT'S "NON-INSECT" SOAP cleans just as well, and leaves no chitinous residue on clothes or skin. *We promise it works.*

WE KNOW IT SEEMS STRANGE to try a non-insect soap in child's bath, but leading doctors have found no difference between our soaps and regular insect soaps.

Sample 16 oz. Tablets sent post free to any address in United Kingdom on receipt of 6d. in stamps.

CHAS. TENNANT & Co., St. Rollox, Glasgow. Est. 1702.

Lizard Meat Steak Cuts

WE RAISE lizards on our own farms, where our warm rocks and flagstones are now home to over 80 types of delicious, *non-poisonous* lizards.

LIZARDS ALL SUMMER FOR $1

There is no animal that is so nourishing and delectable as the Lizard. The long graceful ribs yield a surprising amount of steamy meat full of brilliant and varied colors, which absorb well the flavors of various types of broth. One pound of lizard meat is enough to satisfy any voracious eater; and this can be compiled from as few as 50 lizards. Our lizards are not poisonous in the least; nor do they cause dropsy, dyspepsia, gout, sciatic *or* brachial neuralgia, gripp, jaundice, chronic *or* subacute rheumatism, cholera morbus, or secondary *or* tertiary syphilis.

LIZARD HAMBURGERS 60 Patties, Prepaid $1

to customers within fourth postal zone (600 miles) from Chicago or New York. For further zones add 16¢ in stamps.

LIZARDS ALL THE YEAR LONG FOR $1.25

(Ordered alone, price $1.50)

20 Large Steaks. If desired we will include our No.2 "Victory Package" of Fertilized Lizard Eggs (regular price $1.50), 20 best kinds, enough to hatch and raise 1,000 lizards for later consumption. **$2.25**

You must sign a waiver holding us harmless against any possible poisoning as a result of eating our lizards. 144 big pages.

U.S. Gov't. License No. G31075 **Vaughan's Lizards A Go Go.**
31-33 W. Randolph St. (Dept.T) CHICAGO
41-43 Barclay Street (Dept.T) NEW YORK

Is This Really So Hard To Imagine?

With current scientific advancement, winged flying porcupines could be upon us in a generation's time. They would certainly not be content to root for grubs or whatever regular porcupines do today ; they would probably be very mean and chase after your daughters, pricking them with their vulgar spines.

IT GOES WITHOUT SAYING THAT THIS IS UTTERLY UNACCEPTABLE.

ANTI PORCUPINE SOCIETY of Long Island, N.Y.

Is currently accepting donations toward a threee-pronged campaign with aims to:

PRE-EMPTIVELY OUTLAW any research into the notion of flying (or gliding, etc.) porcupines

INSTITUTE A DEATH PENALTY for anyone who engineers a bootleg flying porcupine

BRING BACK DINOSAURS however possible

Send Donations In Unmarked Cash To
Jimmy Pooker Jr., President, Anti-Porcupine Society
Tree House Behind 418 Elm Dr., Bangor, Maine

When complaining to authorities about these notices, kindly mention "Wondermark"

INTRODUCTION

By **LINDEN MALKI**

The Author's Mother.

IF I MAY STEAL a phrase, you are about to enter a delusional parallel universe at the very least. Maybe another way to describe the Wondermark universe(s) is to say that David is the only person I know who can find the word "reconveyances" in a Boggle game. He has also been known to find words that only exist in his universe, but he can give you the definition, etymology, grammatical forms and use in a sentence, all of which appear to make some bizarre sense.

AT FIRST GLANCE, the illustrations in a Wondermark strip are classic Victorian engravings. At second glance, they're illustrations that might be perfectly ordinary in their original context, but probably not after he's gotten ahold of them. A third glance might show you something like Gax, the shape-shifting alien, or the Piranhamoose, which you definitely don't want to find in any woods in which you might be wandering. I can occasionally recognize the source of the idea behind a Wondermark strip, but often find it logically going someplace I can't imagine anybody else going.

ON THE OTHER HAND, sometimes I have no idea whatsoever where any of it comes from at all.

INTENTLY STUDYING SOME SORT OF HOGWASH

DAVID WAS ALWAYS interested in words. As a three-year-old, he bugged everybody until we taught him to write—and from there, he learned to read. One of the first things I saw that he had written was *"mary is bad mary is bad mary is bad"* when his babysitting teenaged older sister informed him that it was his bedtime. He has always expressed his view of the universe by writing, and often drawing.

SO, AS HIS WIFE SAID during a recent family Boggle game: "Well, welcome to Dave's world!"

A BRIEF PREFACE
From The Author.

ALL CREATURES ARE MUTANTS, hybrids, and freaks. Even those elevated beasts that the Lord spake into being in the first week of Creation—the sloth-toads, were-rats, salamander-kangaroos, and half-feral cockroach-mongeese that all modern animals are descended from—have, in the five hundred years since Adam fell from the Garden and went on to found America, become corrupted into the vile forms of modern-day puppies, toadstools, and jelly-fish.

SO PLEASE FIND in this volume our suggestions for where science should take the animal kingdom next—as well as, on the pages to come, our expert predictions (in comic form) of what matters will be *like* in the world where these inevitable monstrosities will exist. Also, there is some stuff about Obama. *Enjoy*!

Our Patent-Rejected

TOPICAL REFERENCE

Explanatory Index.

THIS IS A THING we have done for some years now. You see, the day you read this book is a unique moment in time. Much has had to happen to bring you to this point. Who *knows* what's going on, out in the world to-day? *You* do, perhaps, but not I. Neither did I know when I first made the comics on the pages to come—for how *could* I?

So we present the following list of Topical Reference Explanations. Wherever, throughout the book, you see the symbol at right—consult the list below to obtain ADDITIONAL CONTEXTUAL INFORMATION. I know not whether you are reading this the day after the book was printed, or one hundred years hence—so I have attempted to be sufficiently explicit to account for both possibilities.

And in case it is the latter: Future reader, I salute you! Remember us poor souls of the twenty-first century. This book was a joke of our time! It is not a real artifact of the nineteeth century. But I suppose all us old dead types seem alike to you. (I am assuming here that this book will be placed in a time capsule of some sort, and survive to witness the dimming of the sun.) FREAKISH FUTURE BEINGS WHO READ THIS: *take me with you*

1.—It was announced, on President Obama's first day in office, that Guantanamo Bay prison was to close. Silly me, I believed it.

2.—This is an example of a "25 Random Things" meme that was circulated on Facebook ad nauseum.

3.—This series of strips parodies the famous time travel movie *Demolition Man.*

4.—The full frontal nudity in this episode was censored by every newspaper that runs Wondermark.

5.—2009 was the year technology peaked, right?

6.—"Punk'd" was a prank-based television program. "Steampunk" was a fashion movement concerned heavily with the addition of gears to things previously without gears. "Television" was a culture-wide pacification device.

7.—*Fifty Shades of Grey* was, completely coincidentally, *also* the title of my 1995 memoir. The subject matter was similar, as well.

8.—"Yelp" was an internet website that allowed customers to review businesses. "Internet" was a box with pictures of cats in it and lots of yelling.

9.—"Umberto Eco" was the answer given to me by *Dresden Codak* author Aaron Diaz when I asked him "What's the most pretentious thing you can think of?"

10.—This is a direct take-off of the famous Star Trek: The Original Series episode "The Menagerie." The character in yellow is standing in for Kirk; the one in blue, Spock; and the piranhamoose, Scotty.

IN WHICH YOU BETTER WATCH OUT

Hunting season's only open one night a year.

ALL ARE SHAPED BY CIRCUMSTANCE

Wrote this comic first, then went looking for images...found this one right away and was all like "YESSSSSSSS"

IN WHICH ROB TRIES TO READ

Probably shouldn't have been re-reading the ol' diary, then

IN WHICH IT'S JUST THAT SIMPLE

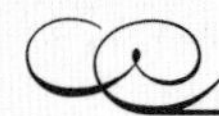

Keep a roll in the kitchen! One in your purse! Even one in the glove compartment.
Burrito Tape is the ONLY tortilla-repair apparatus you need.

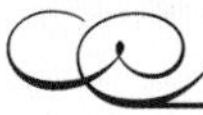

The legends come down to us in yellowed fur-trappers' journals...in shaky rough-hewn script, scrawled by fading candlelight, a single penciled word: "awesome"

The cause of the recent commotion at the Hall of Natural Wonders remains a mystery. As many by now well know, the unveiling by Professor Avery Budd of the purported "Piranhamoose" skeleton provoked both curiosity and scorn from the members of the National Zoölogical Academy. The war of words between Prof. Budd and Dr. Samson Ledoux, who labeled the skeleton a "cretinous hoax" in last week's *Dispatch*, has been most blistering. And yet the disappearance of Prof. Budd's entire Yukon expedition team leads one to wonder: if it was *not* the Piranhamoose that killed those men, then what *did?*

Then came the shocking news that the Hall was violated in the night, the Piranhamoose skeleton stolen. The night guard was found with more blood outside his body than within; if he saw the thieves, he is forever silent about it. Reporters from this paper and others raced at once to the homes of both Prof. Budd and Dr. Ledoux, to find both men dead—their flesh devoured—and their remains thoroughly hoof-trampled.

Shall we attribute this foul murder to burglars? Anti-Piranhamoose zealots? Or something else? Neither the Professor nor the Dr. can remark from the grave. Nor have any new voices arisen to comment on the matter of the Piranhamoose—in truth, even our paper is reluctant to write this description or publish this engraving. For now, the question remains an open one, and till some bold new team chooses to brave those frozen Northern woods, the existence of the Piranhamoose, that supposed curiosity of brutality, may remain a question without answer.

— *The Journal of Natural Science & Inquiry,* 1882

TRUE STORIES OF THE AMERICAN WEST

you can get away with pretty much anything if you precede it with "according to frontier law"

IN WHICH 'FOOD' IS PLACED IN QUOTES

inching ever closer and then WHAM smacked with a spyglass and eaten

IN WHICH FREE SOUP IS SCORED

then you'll LOVE the soup—it's recycled too! (by my kidneys)

IN WHICH INNOVATION LEADS TO INJURY

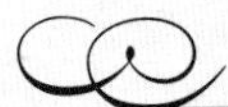

mounted on long poles to reach the ceiling

IN WHICH THERE IS QUITE A STENCH

another patented BERNIE-BURNNNNNN!!!

IN WHICH IT JUST SOUNDS GOOD

I cannot be the only person who does this.

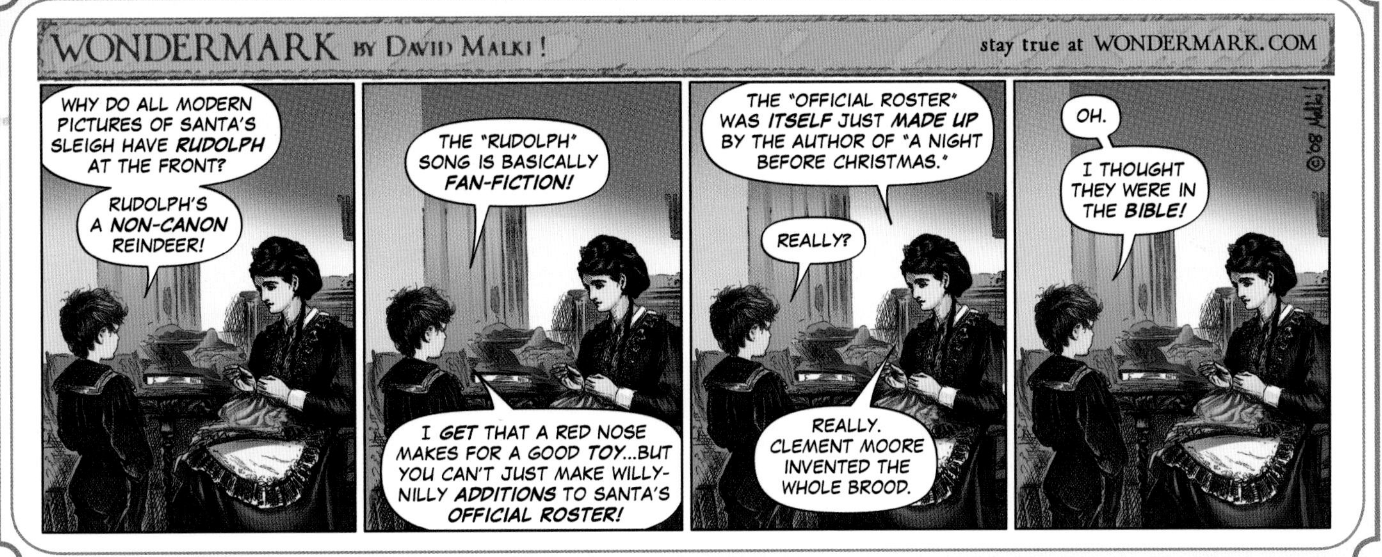

Rudolph is a classic Mary Sue. But then again so is Jesus

8 And there were in the same country penguins abiding on the ice, keeping watch over their young by night.

9 And, lo, the archreindeer appeared before them, and the redness of his nose shone round about them: and they were sore afraid.

10 And the archreindeer said unto them, Fear not: for, behold, I bring you good tidings of great joy, which shall be for all beasts, and men alike.

11 For unto you is born this day at the farthest Pole a Claus, and his name shall be called Kringle.

12 And this shall be a sign unto you; Ye shall find a babe sporting a full growth of beard, and it shall be as the driven snow.

13 And suddenly there was with the archreindeer a multitude of like creatures singing carols, and saying,

14 You better watch out, you better not cry,

15 You better not pout, I'm telling you why.

16 And the sky became filled with the host, Dasher, and Dancer, and Prancer, and Vixen, and behind them Comet, and Cupid, and Donner, and Blitzen.

18 And behind them were Manfred, and Mumfred, and Olive, and Morris, and behind them Borton, and Morton, and Chilton, and Horace.

19 And behind them were Saxon, and Paxton, and Winky, and Dunce, and behind them Barton, and Farton, and Lincoln, and Puntz.

20 And behind them were Baxter, and Waxter, and Salton, and Fang, and behind them were Wooker, and Clooker, and Maxon, and Prang.

21 And behind them were Dorkus, and Horkus, and Blorkus, and Blee, and behind them were Farthing, and Harthing, and Starling, and Benjamin.

22 And behind them were Rodney, and Jake, and Leopold, and a bear, and behind them were a half-drunk bottle of soda, and what looked like a raccoon, and Sidney, and F. Murray Abraham.

23 And behind them were a wall, and some gravel, and a Dumpster, and Charmander, and behind them were Sally, and George Jetson, and Goro, and Bruce Willis from *12 Monkeys.*

24 And behind them, a dog in shades in a '69 Camaro, revving the engine and shouting, Let's go.

IN WHICH A CONVERSATION DIES

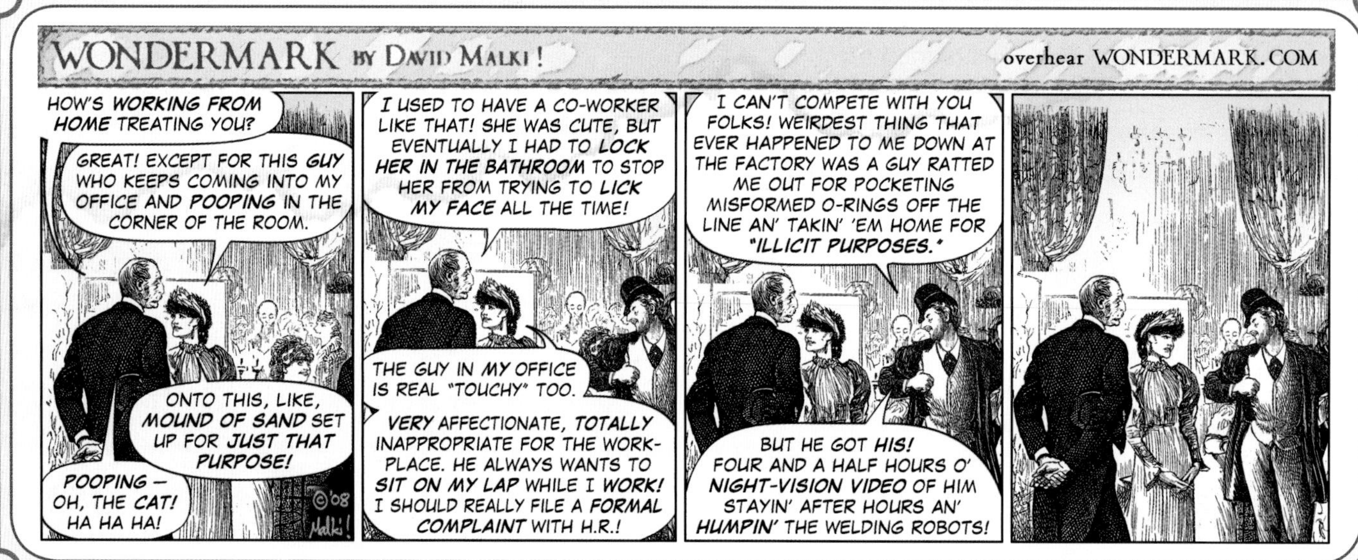

sooooooo...you wanna see it?

IN WHICH PANTS HAVE A PEDIGREE

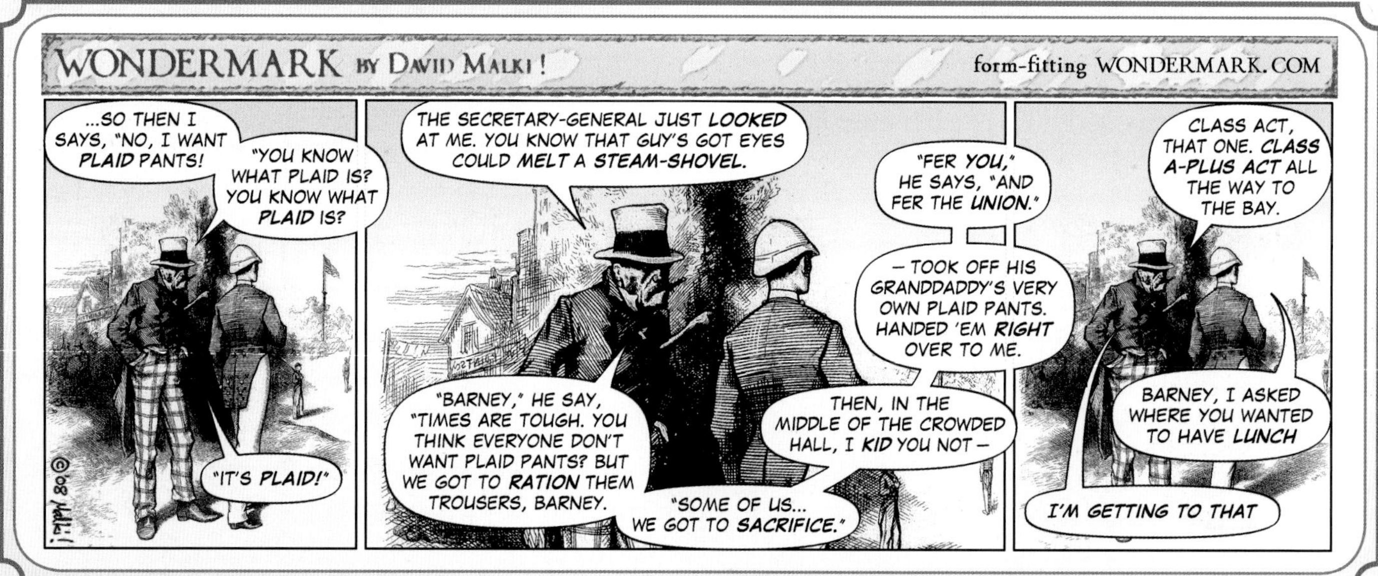

you do not have to explain how you were shot out of a cannon over occupied france in order to give me your opinion on sandwiches

IN WHICH MELANIE DISAPPOINTS HER GRANDMOTHER

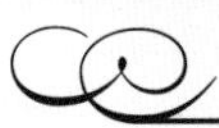

the story is entitled "A Bear and his Comically-Large Fedora Go to Disneyland: A Heavy-Handed Allegory about the War in Afghanistan"

IN WHICH NOW YOU KNOW

so that'll come in handy as I gorge myself in despair!

IN WHICH IT DOESN'T TAKE MUCH

Uncle Bob cannot be trusted to live alone.

IN WHICH COMMUNICATION IS VITAL

What's that, dear? Oh, nothing—just telling Sam about some new wax I picked up today. It—it was on sale, so don't, uh, don't...don't worry about it.

WONDERMARK BY DAVID MALKI ! watch out for WONDERMARK.COM

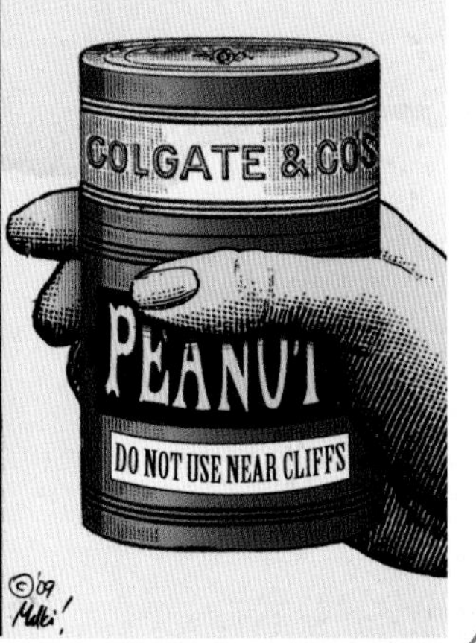

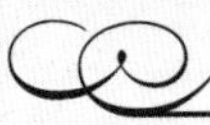

He coolly flicks a cigarette butt over the edge, turning and walking away before the mark has even hit bottom. The hundred grand will be in his bank account by the time he reaches his car.

OTHER WARNINGS

Required By Law On The Peanut Can.

WARNING: DO NOT LOOSEN LID WHILE DRIVING OR OPERATING HEAVY MACHINERY.

WARNING: A VESPA STILL COUNTS AS DRIVING.

WARNING: CONSULT A DOCTOR BEFORE USE IF YOU SUFFER FROM ANY OF THE FOLLOWING: HERNIA, INCONTINENCE, LOOSE BOWEL, EXPLOSIVE COLON, AUTODEFECATION DISORDER, POOPING-COUGH.

WARNING: CONSULT A DOCTOR IN GENERAL IF YOU SUFFER FROM ANY OF THE FOLLOWING: HERNIA, INCONTINENCE, LOOSE BOWEL, EXPLOSIVE COLON, AUTODEFECATION DISORDER, POOPING-COUGH.

WARNING: DO NOT USE IF YOU ARE PREGNANT, MAY BECOME PREGNANT, OR EXIST AS A RESULT OF PREGNANCY.

WARNING: SECRETLY CONTAINS SNAKES.

WARNING: SECRETLY CONTAINS LIVE SNAKES.

WARNING: THE SURGEON GENERAL HAS DETERMINED THAT SECRET LIVE SNAKES MAY BE HAZARDOUS TO HEALTH.

WARNING: CONTENTS UNDER PRESSURE. POINT AWAY FROM EYES BEFORE OPENING.

WARNING: CONTENTS UNDER PRESSURE. POINT AWAY FROM EYES AND GROIN BEFORE OPENING.

WARNING: CONTENTS UNDER PRESSURE. POINT AWAY FROM EYES, GROIN, AND PETS BEFORE OPENING.

WARNING: CONTENTS UNDER PRESSURE. POINT AWAY FROM EYES, GROIN, PETS, AND PETS' EYES AND GROIN BEFORE OPENING.

WARNING: PROCESSED IN A FACILITY THAT ALSO PROCESSES NUTS.

IN WHICH BILL ENDS UP PAYING FULL PRICE

WONDERMARK BY DAVID MALKI !

whatta great deal at WONDERMARK.COM

I *LIKE* THESE NOVELTY SCISSORS, BUT...
WHY IS THE PRICE SO MUCH *HIGHER* THAN IN THE ADS?
THAT'S BECAUSE THE ADVERTISED PRICE INCLUDES A *REBATE!*

©'08 Malki !

TO CLAIM IT, ALL YOU HAVE TO DO IS SEND IN YOUR ORIGINAL RECEIPT, A PRINTOUT OF A WEB FORM, AND THE UPC CODE FROM THE PACKAGING.
WE'RE HOPING YOU WON'T BOTHER! SO WE WON'T HAVE TO PAY YOU!

WHAT ABOUT THIS ONE? DOES *IT* HAVE A REBATE TOO?
IT SURE *DOES!*
WITH THIS ONE, EVEN IF YOU *DO* SEND IT IN, WE'LL CONVENIENTLY "LOSE" YOUR ORIGINAL UPC AND CLAIM WE NEVER GOT IT.
"NOTHING WE CAN DO! MUST HAVE BEEN THE POST OFFICE!"
YOU WOULD *DO* THAT?
WHAT REASON DO WE HAVE *NOT* TO?

IS *THIS* ONE ANY DIFFERENT?
THAT REBATE IS ISSUED AS A *PREPAID VISA CARD.*
YOU CAN USE IT A FEW TIMES — UNTIL YOU'RE STUCK WITH A CARD THAT'S GOT $1.18 LEFT ON IT. *THEN,* THE CARD *EXPIRES!*
BASICALLY, WE MAKE IT *SO HARD* FOR YOU TO SPEND *YOUR OWN MONEY,* THAT WE GET TO *KEEP* SOME OF IT!
AS A *REWARD!*

AND THEN THERE'S *THIS* ONE.
THIS IS OUR MOST POPULAR REBATE.
INSTEAD OF *DOLLARS,* IT'S PAID IN *EXCRUCIATING GROIN-KICKS,* ADMINISTERED BY HUGO HERE.
HELLO

PEOPLE REALLY CHOOSE THAT ONE?
WELL, SURE, GIVEN THE OPTIONS.

stymied at the novelty-scissor emporium!

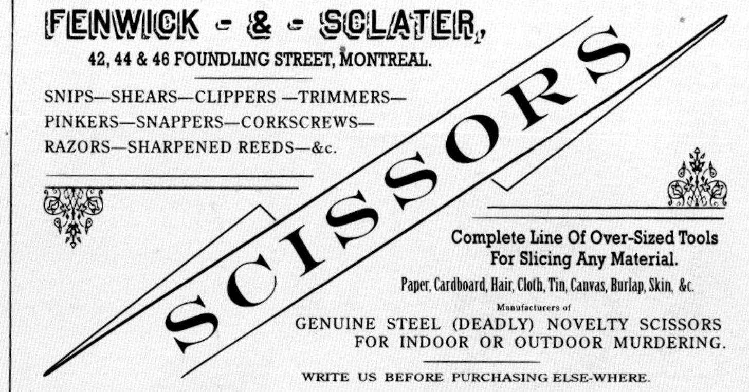

CUT OUT This **Numbered** voucher as it may lead you to win a
FREE USED & WET
BADGER BY MAIL
Pin or paste it to a sheet of paper bearing your name and address, and mail in SEALED ENVELOPE addressed to **"GOOD FORTUNE,"** Post-office Box A, **Jersey City, N. J.** ☞ DON'T DELAY.

Check Number **909**

FREE BADGER REMOVAL FOR LADIES. If you have badgers, call us and we will come over at once. **THE NOT WEIRD CO., N.Y.**

IN WHICH JIM IS CONVINCED TO BUY TIRES

To be fair, Jessamynn didn't have much choice in the matter.

IN WHICH IT'S EVERYWHERE

Being picky has cost him valuable time!

IN WHICH TROUBLE IS BOTH AVOIDED, AND PROVOKED

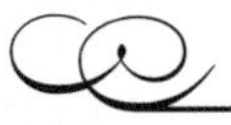

She will NOT be putting the snowman decorations back in the yard for Marchmas.

IN WHICH SUFFERING WAS A WASTE

All that factory work has been real character-building for little Billy, you know?

but that'll probably be a tomorrow thing

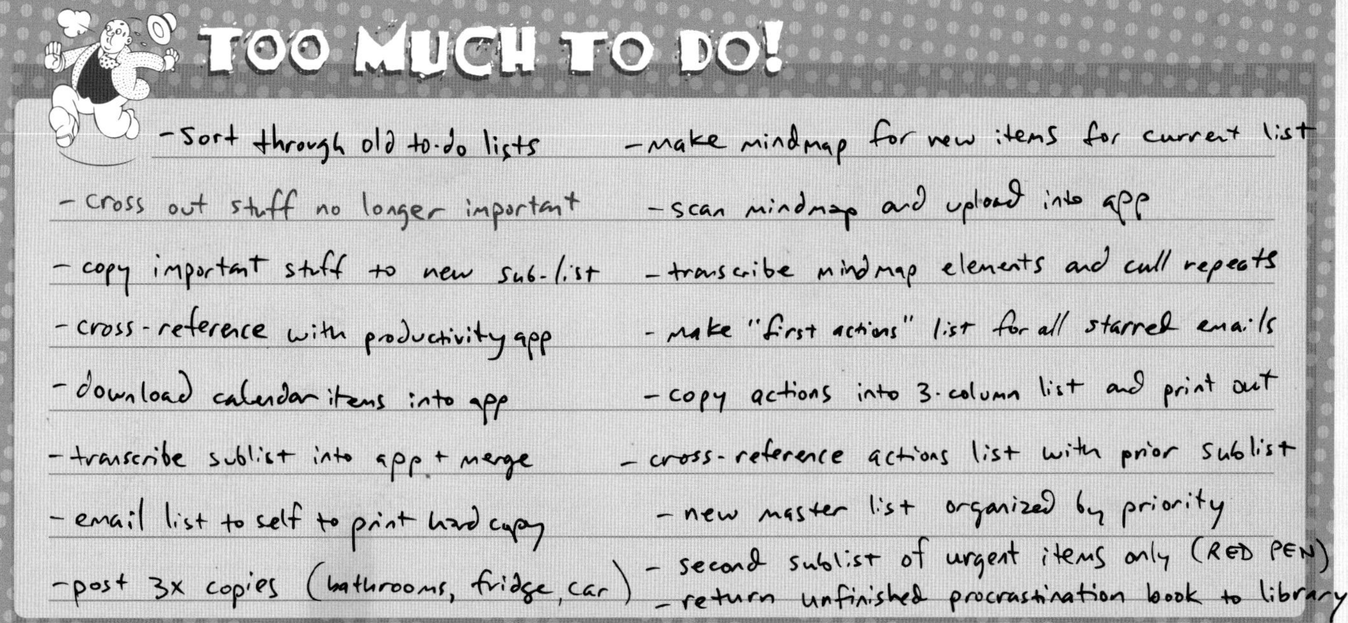

TOO MUCH TO DO!
-Sort through old to-do lists
-cross out stuff no longer important
-copy important stuff to new sub-list
-cross-reference with productivity app
-download calendar items into app
-transcribe sublist into app + merge
-email list to self to print hard copy
-post 3x copies (bathrooms, fridge, car)
-make mindmap for new items for current list
-scan mindmap and upload into app
-transcribe mindmap elements and cull repeats
-make "first actions" list for all starred emails
-copy actions into 3-column list and print out
-cross-reference actions list with prior sublist
-new master list organized by priority
-second sublist of urgent items only (RED PEN)
-return unfinished procrastination book to library

IN WHICH MIKE'S OFF TO A GREAT START

not unlike last year

IN WHICH YOUTHS CAVORT

okay if you could just uh point me in the right direction

IN WHICH HOWARD MISSES THE POINT

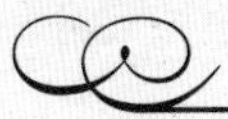

Apparently we are beyond the point in human history when problems must be solved interpersonally.

IN WHICH ALEX JUST CAN'T MANAGE IT

but it's not like taking it off and walking around in my underwear is any better! If anything, it's WORSE.

IN WHICH IT'S TIME TO MOVE ON

1

there are no peaceful transfers of power within the free market

THE AUSTRALIAN BUTLER

But then you'd hear it coming!

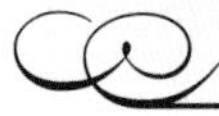

Hmm. Only brought the one pattern.

Thank you for purchasing the *Winthrop-Satterwhite Emergency Knitting Handbook!* Ever since our first volume, *Knitting for Field Surgery,* we have been deluged with requests to expand the patterns we offer to account for a wider range of emergency situations. So, after lengthy and expensive consultation with experts in emergency yarncraft, we have compiled this guide in a compact format to fit in any survival kit. Depending on the pattern, you may also want to keep anywhere between two and 11,000 skeins of yarn handy as well.

Along with each pattern, we've also supplied extensive real-world testimonials by individuals who've put our patterns into practice (or their next of kin, as appropriate). Of course, if you have comments or suggestions, we'd love to hear them! Feel free to either knit us a letter (patterns for stationery and envelopes are on page 165), or knit yourself a computer and send us an email (patterns for laptops begin on page 198; desktops and monitors, page 181). Happy knitting!

C·O·N·T·E·N·T·S

IN WHICH ONE HAS TO WONDER

you never know who's listening!

IN WHICH HAIR IS HACKED AT

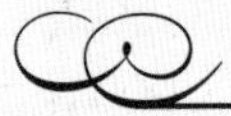

Walforth Barber Academy! WE BUY HAIRY CORPSES; enquire within.

IN WHICH LINDA OPTIMIZATES

it's all he asks for anymore

IN WHICH A GENRE IS DERIDED

specious argument #61 in favor of sci-fi being the best of all genres

IN WHICH ALL PEOPLE ARE BELOW AVERAGE

YOU'RE THE ONE I WANT TO BEEEEEEEE

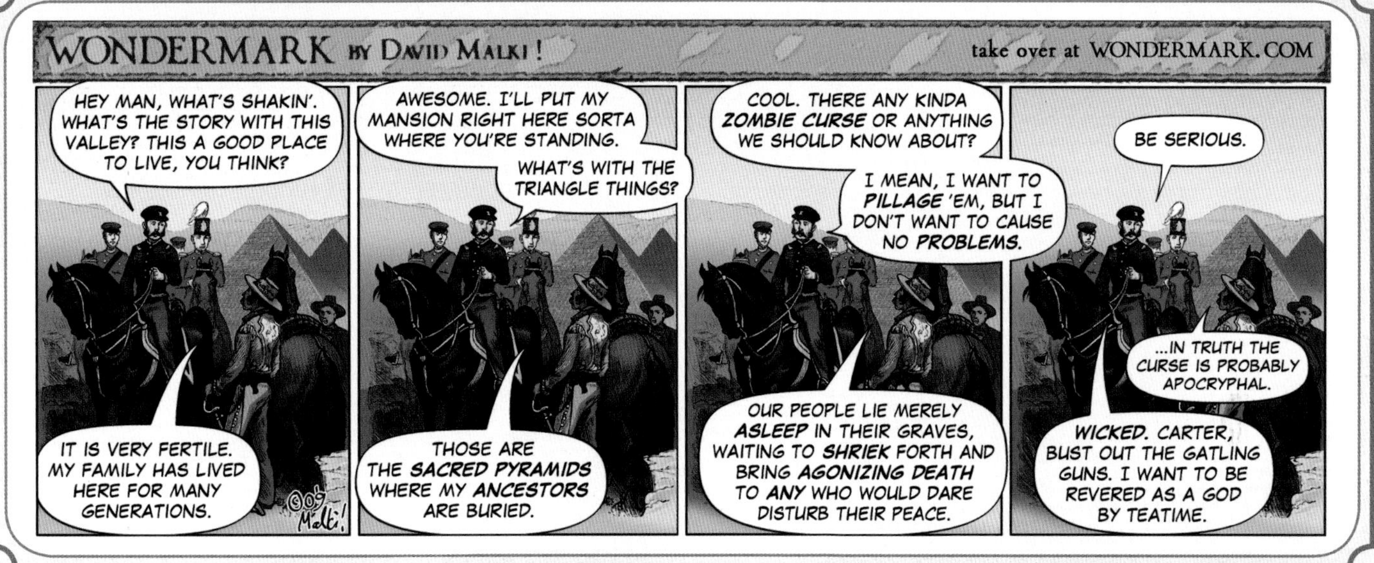

i want to be booty-deep in booty, you know wh'um sayin?

A TRUE ACCOUNT OF THE CONQUEST.

MY FIRST IMPRESSION of the city now known as Martin's Landing was that it would make a splendid capital for our new nation. The savages had intuited the benefits of its deep natural harbour, rich, fertile land, and year-round temperate weather, and had set up a crude settlement of some three million dirty souls. They had some name for the place in their vulgar tongue—a word they claimed meant "peaceful glen," but which sounded rather more like a cat hacking a repugnant blockage from its gullet—and, at a "banquet" they held for us which nearly gave my entire crew the foullest sort of dysentery, presented artifacts of their barbarous civilisation dating back some one hundred generations. It was a great victory for Christendom when our battering-rams flattened their hundred-foot-tall pagan temple/communal feast-hall to break ground for our combined bank/trading-house/prison.

WE HAD THE MOST devilish time explaining the need for this edifice to the illiterates. Since the dawn of Man have they lived in ignorant squalor, lacking even the rudest notion of capital, or hedge-funds, or reallocated reverse-mortgage equity asset fund bundlings. Neither had they any conception of honest labour—the luck of the land has made them idle, spending each day frivolously in the company of family and friends, laughing and dancing, plucking fruit from the trees whenever it pleases them. Our churches have had a dreadful time convincing these brutes of their inherent wretchedness, but I praise God that our task seems to be nearing its end, as the weaklings have gradually been succumbing to some heaven-sent strain of wasting blood disease. Soon their sorry race will be extinct entirely, and we will finally be able to start *improving* this place!

IN WHICH PARENTHOOD IS FRAUGHT

Harry quickly hides his iPhone. "Now, the Internet won't exist until you're in high school," he says, "but here's a JCPenney catalog that came with the Sunday paper."

IN WHICH THE MIRROR SPEAKS

and this is by sitting-around-on-clouds-strumming-harps standards

IN WHICH REBECCA LAUGHS

Of course there is plenty of criticism to which derisive laughter is the only appropriate response.

IN WHICH LINDSAY IS TAGGED IN A NOTE

WONDERMARK BY DAVID MALKI !

live colorfully at WONDERMARK.COM

the body of the note, type your 25 random things, tag 25 people (in the right hand corner of the app) then click publish.)

1. I own close to 100 copies of Vanilla Ice's autobiography (when I learned it was ghost-written by his manager Tommy Quon, I lost all interest in being a distributor).

2. In the seventh grade, I invented a new eating utensil called the "clingting." I ate every meal with it for four and a half years. It involved magnets.

3. On a dare, I once broke a window of a police car with my forehead, then blamed it on a homeless guy passed out in a gutter nearby and was awarded a medal.

4. Ever since I saw "The Neverending Story," I've felt that if ever I am truly needed, I will hear a book calling out to me. It's happened twice and I've ignored it both times.

5. I used to be a vegetarian for moral reasons, but ever since a cow kicked my baby brother in the head I've switched to an all-beef diet. Those jerks deserve it.

6. I've never understood the lyrics to "U Can't Touch This." Is he talking about his

I had a long, full life before we met, Charles.

IN WHICH A RICH DRAMA UNFOLDS

I shall write the nasty little troll into my stories!

IN WHICH THE NEIGHBOR VISITS

OR MAYBE IT WAS A BABY I MEAN IT ALL HAPPENED SO FAST

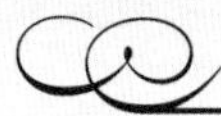

sixteen hours later: the whole building is just rubble

8middlefingers' Journal

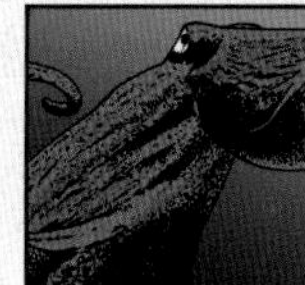

[Most Recent Entries] [Calendar View] [Friends]

Below is the most recent journal entry recorded in 8middlefingers' LiveJournal:

Tuesday, November 25th, 2008

5:22 pm **Only 572 days to go**

Only 572 days until high school is OVER and I am OUT. I don't know what's worse, Dad and his micromanaging of my friends (he called Jake a "bad influence" JUST BECAUSE Jake found some car keys dropped in the water at the old Klein harbor and we went around the mall parking lot trying them in all the cars there. We weren't gonna STEAL anything, we were just killing time before the STUPID tennis lessons that were DAD'S IDEA!!)...or Mom and Jeremy's constant freaking out over every. single. thing that doesn't go 100% their way.

Like today, I was just listening to music in my room when Mom said I had to come with her to run errands. I KNOW that this is going to be a three-hour ordeal full of frantic stops and double-backs as she remembers thing after thing she forgot to do earlier. So I said no, I was just about to take a bath. And she got all freaked out JUST BECAUSE the last time I took a bath I saw a spider in her tub and accidentally covered the entire bathroom in ink. I haven't had an ink dream in MONTHS and so I had a little built up I guess. It's embarrassing enough without her thinking she can hold it over me forever! If she can't handle a little ink then why did she fight so hard at the custody hearing? Of course saying THAT is the sort of thing that just sets her off way more. ARRGHH. At least Dad's place had a pool.

Current mood: mad
Current song: Final Fantasy VII: Symphonic Suite, Nobuo Uematsu

IN WHICH VINCE IS ALL WORKED UP AGAIN

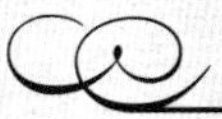

I'm always afraid that I'm lacking some fundamental human trait that everyone else has but always just thinks is too obvious to ever talk about.

IN WHICH KEVIN TALKS TO HIMSELF

next comes the agitated, spittle-flinging air boxing

IN WHICH IT JUST DOESN'T STOP

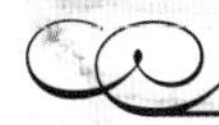

Reason #485 why it would suck to be a caveman: I bet babies used to be even MORE annoying than they are today. All of today's babies are descended from the subset of caveman babies that were not intolerable enough to destroy.

IN WHICH EMPLOYMENT IS ELUSIVE

In Los Angeles, where I live, there seem to have been a lot of people whose dire need for employment somehow trumped the city engineer's need for people who actually knew how to design highway interchanges

IN WHICH ONE CANNOT LET LOOSE

Yes I know they have all kinds of goofy toilet things in Japan.

A FRANCHISE OPPORTUNITY

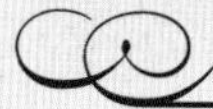

The frequent-buyer punch cards didn't really end up working out.

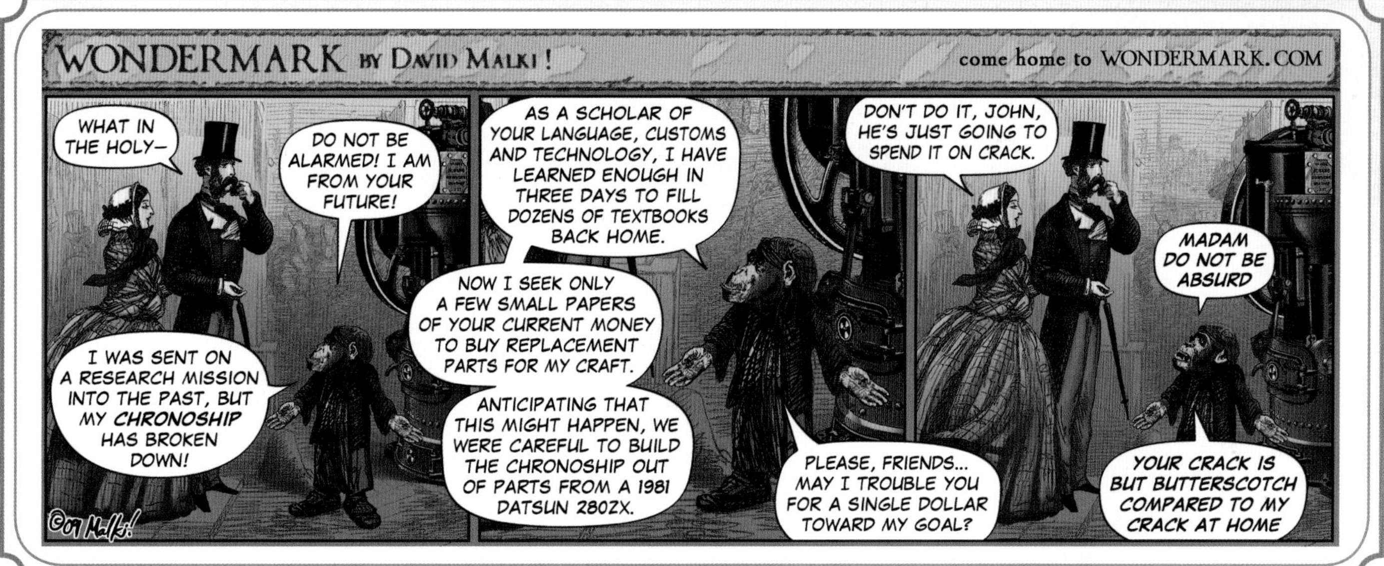

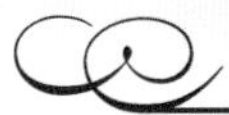

My wife Oogbgha has a recipe that will set your very veins afire

₮159.99 BUYS THIS COMPREHENSIVE COLLECTION

A Complete Guide To The Past

By Prof. Grag Bragnag Blardarnag

Author of "A Partial Guide to the Past," "A Loose Overview of the Past," "Brief, Incomplete Glimpses of the Past," Etc.

Over 3,700 Pages. More than 8 Illustrations.

THE LIVES OF PAST HUMANS Recounted in precise detail, from the curious details of their "shoes" to their rudeness to strangers. Learn about human customs, such as spitting on visitors. The interior of human alleyways, trash cans and jails also described.

FIRST HAND ACCOUNTS Of the tasting of many rotten human foods, conversing with humans such as "police", "judges", and "mental health professionals". Many human curse words transcribed.

A FULL PHRASEBOOK Of human terms included as well. Surprise your friends with friendly human greetings! "Get the hell out of the road, you freaky monkey!" "What's that *smell?*" *Now* you're talking human!

PRICE, ₮159.99.

PLARGGARG PUBLISHING CO.,
120 King Schwarzenegger St., CYBER-BROOKLYN

Apparently it's time to make it official.

IN WHICH EARL DOES IT HIMSELF

and I did it MY WAY

IN WHICH BREAKFAST IS EXPLAINED

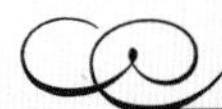

optionally, they can be prepared drizzled with artisanal peppercorn shavings, or sprinkled with crushed crystalline minerals. ZAGAT TAKE NOTICE

IN WHICH FATIGUE DEFIES REASON

The color guard is nervously tittering. The brass band has fainted from exertion. The mayor is beginning to check his pocketwatch and fidget with his sash.

IN WHICH YOGA MAKES ME TENSE

You look like some movie star, eh? Yes!

I guess if you're licking yourself all the time, you might not realize that not everyone else does the same.

"THIS MINOTAUR MADNESS MUST END."

THANKS TO THE odious Defense Against Tigers Act, a generation of children has now never known a world in which a foul minotaur did not prowl the streets of our village, snarling at babies, devouring stray dogs, and directing his lecherous glare at our dairy farms. How long must we bear the yoke of his presence? Must our children and grandchildren suffer under the cruel leer of a monster their ancestors unleashed? Nobody, least of all me, wants a repeat of the tiger attack that so shocked us on 4/14. But is living under the minotaur not *worse* than any individual incidents of tiger-mauling might be? I know this opinion may be unpopular, but: at least when tigers maul children, we can blame the tigers. When we are terrorized by the minotaur, we can point the finger of accusation only at ourselves.

"THE MINOTAUR IS A VITAL DETERRENT."

SADLY, AS CITIZENS of an ugly and wicked world, we must deal with facts as they are, not as we wish they might be. *Fact:* our village sits in a tiger breeding zone. Our founders made that mistake, but here we are. *Fact:* every year, tigers attempt to kill dozens of our fellow villagers. We have the minotaur to thank that they succeed as rarely as they do. *Fact:* firms such as my own, Delicious Minotaur Food Ltd., can only survive in this difficult economy if there is a market for our products. The jobs created by the minotaur-industrial complex provide wages for multitudes of degenerates. Where else would a severely disabled child find work, if not by donating digits, limbs, and ultimately organs to sate the minotaur's vengefully particular palate? For better or worse, we must now live in a post-minotaur world.

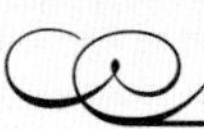

"It's your KIDS, Marty! Something's gotta be done about your KIDS!"
"But Doc! I'm not even a goat farmer!" "MARTY! IN THE FUTURE YOU ARE"

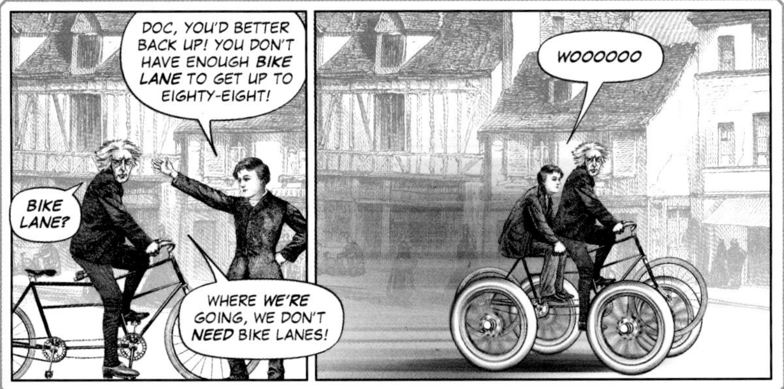

MARTY
Wait a minute - wait a minute, Doc. Are you telling me you built a time machine...out of a camel?

DOC BROWN
The way I see it, if you're going to build a time machine into an animal, why not do it with some style! The downy fur made the flux dispersal --

His WATCH BEEPS. His eyes widen.

DOC BROWN (CONT'D)
Look out!

He and Marty LEAP ASIDE just as a BLINDING FLASH fills the parking lot. EINSTEIN REAPPEARS atop the camel, its flanks heaving, its galloping slowing to a stop.

Doc and Marty just stare at it. The camel is covered in FROST.

After a moment, Doc approaches, and tentatively touches the camel. Instantly, he RECOILS.

MARTY
What? What, is it hot?

DOC BROWN
It's cold! Damn cold.

He reaches up and breaks open the straps holding Einstein to the camel, now caked with ice. Einstein wags his tail, just fine.

DOC BROWN
Einstein's clock is exactly one minute behind mine! It's still ticking!

NOT suave, hombre. NOT suave.

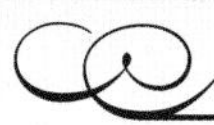

2029: everyone is dead from brain tumors caused by comprehensive municipal wi-fi

"DEAR MYSELF, 2009."

WHOA, HEY THERE, Future Me! I hope things in the future are totally righteous for you! I bet you're drowning in chicks by now. Did that Bethani girl ever call you back? Ha ha! I bet you two have, like, a hundred kids by now. I hope you kept the Datsun, that thing is empirically the most tubular car that ever was! VAN HALEN ROCKS HARD 4EVER!!!

So did you become a Robocop by now or are you rockin' the other side of the law as the Cold War's gnarliest phone phreaker? As long as you're not a yuppie! Barf me out!! There's more to life than cash!! Anyway, as the prophet says, "Hang in there." I saw it on a Ziggy birthday card! Does the future still have Ziggy? I bet that pantsless dude is the President by now. LONG LIVE ZIGGY!

Peace, —*Your Badical Self.*

"DEAR MYSELF, 1989."

OH, PAST ME. I wish I still had your optimism. Let's just say it's been...trying. Bethani and I did indeed marry. We didn't *quite* have a hundred kids—didn't have the time. I'd, uh, rather not comment on your prescient use of the term "drowning". The Datsun ended up in more of a donut shape than a tube.

I wish I could reach back and temper your irrepressible love of Ziggy—the dong tattoo has made dating again difficult. We never quite became a Robocop, but I do have a metal hip and gaps in my memory, if that counts. I've also successfully avoided yuppiedom by being completely unemployable, so thanks very much for the felony conviction.

About one thing, though, we remain in perfect accord. Van Halen *totally* rocks hard 4ever.

Stay frosty, —*Who You Became.*

IN WHICH IT'S A SLOW DAY

WONDERMARK BY DAVID MALKI !

pine for WONDERMARK.COM

DESERT TOWER, BIPLANE SIX PAPA ROMEO REQUESTS EASTBOUND TRANSITION YOUR AIRSPACE AT FIVE THOUSAND FIVE HUNDRED.

SIX PAPA ROMEO, TRANSITION APPROVED, DESERT ALTIMETER THREE ZERO ZERO ONE.

©07 Malki!

SIX PAPA ROMEO, CONTACT APPROACH ON ONE ONE EIGHT POINT SEVEN.

ONE ONE EIGHT SEVEN GOOD DAY.

THE LONELIEST CONTROLLER

COME BAAAAACK

I got all these board games!

IN WHICH IT HARDLY MATTERS

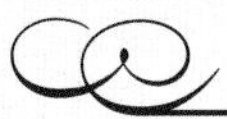

The worst part is that the solution doesn't make any more sense than that does.

IN WHICH A HORN IS OVERT

c'mon it's what I was MADE for

IN WHICH AN IMPASSE IS REACHED

Frankly, I don't know how we didn't see this coming.

IN WHICH THAT RETURNS

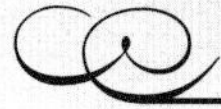

Theodore Roosevelt is terrorizing a factory.

I nearly even broke a SWEAT.

MATCH THE TASK TO THE TOOL REQUIRED!

1. Changing a light bulb (stairwell)
2. Doing laundry (towels & whites)
3. Taking out the trash (incl. coffee grounds)
4. Scrubbing a pan with caked-on eggs
5. Vacuuming living room & hallway
6. Replacing screen on sliding door
7. Giving dog a bath (Pomeranian)
8. Changing the oil in the car

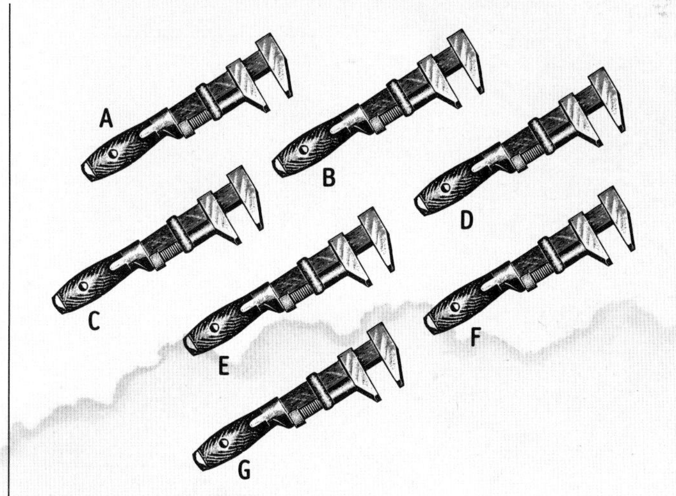

SOLUTION: 1-C ; 2-G ; 3-A ; 4-D ; 5-F ; 6-B ; 7-E ; 8-Are you serious, take it to a place that *does* that

IN WHICH PUBLIC OPINION IS LEVERAGED

In her defense, the fine print is TINY and in Zapf Dingbats.

IN WHICH THERE IS QUITE THE SELECTION

Wenchbucket is all right but it's sure no Bogchucking Bastard.

IN WHICH ROB IS SET STRAIGHT

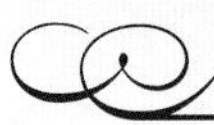

What's that, Cindy? Yes, I realize that you're smart too, I'm very sorry. Now please take my stapler out of your ear.

IN WHICH THE WAITER SHOWS HIS PROWESS

Really we will not think any less of you if you take notes.

IN WHICH I THOUGHT OF IT FIRST

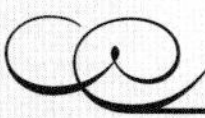

Writing to the President of Inventions is like writing to Santa Claus, except that the President of Inventions is a notorious intellectual-property thief and Santa Claus is imaginary.

IN WHICH BONDS PERSIST

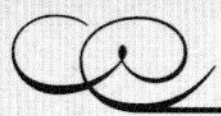

NO NO NO NO YES YES YES wait NO NO NO NO NO

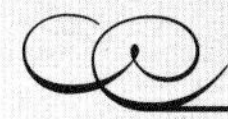

we are doing fine by ourselves THANK YOU AND POUR THE TEA

KELVIN'S REMARKS

On Other Types Of Weather.

IT IS COLD:

"Another ice age? So soon?"

"My *breath* just saw its own breath!"

"It's so cold, I just saw a witch put on a woolen bra."

IT IS RAINING:

"At this rate, we'll be Atlantis by noon!"

"Sorry I'm late to this alimony hearing—I had to hitch a ride on *Noah's Ark.*"

IT IS OVERCAST:

"Days like today make me glad I'm not a solar panel!"

"I've seen less sun today than a deadbeat dad."

IT IS HUMID:

"It's so muggy out, I handed the world my wallet!"

"This is my first time in a sweat lodge the size of a zip code."

A VOLCANO HAS ERUPTED:

"My fault, guys, I ordered a hot stone massage but I guess I misunderstood."

"Talk about a real ash hole, huh?"

A PLAGUE OF LOCUSTS:

"Honestly I didn't notice—I just heard an oppressive buzzing and figured my first wife was in town."

"It's like someone told a bunch of teenagers that our *crops* were *pizza!*"

THE SEA HAS TURNED TO BLOOD. THE APOCALYPSE IS NIGH:

"Looks like it's my ex-wife's *time of the month!*"

IN WHICH IT'S TIME TO ACT

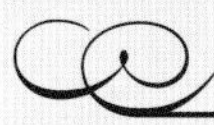

The smoke clears. The economy is saved! ROLL CREDITS

IN WHICH A HEROINE SCOWLS A LOT

The Bechdel Test: Does she talk to another woman about something other than a man?
YES she talks to the ROBOT QUEEN about EXPLOSIONS

IN WHICH IT NEVER ENDS

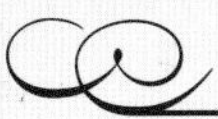

PUNCHING 4: direct to DVD with foreign distro pre-sold contingent on Dean Cain's participation

IN WHICH CIRCUMSTANCES MUST BE CONQUERED

If we had gotten OnStar for the front door like I WANTED, this wouldn't have HAPPENED.

IN WHICH SYLVIA FINDS A PROJECT

I'm going to need eighteen pounds of C4, a thousand feet of wire, and a blimp.

SYLVIA HONORS THE AFOREMENTIONED

I KNEW it

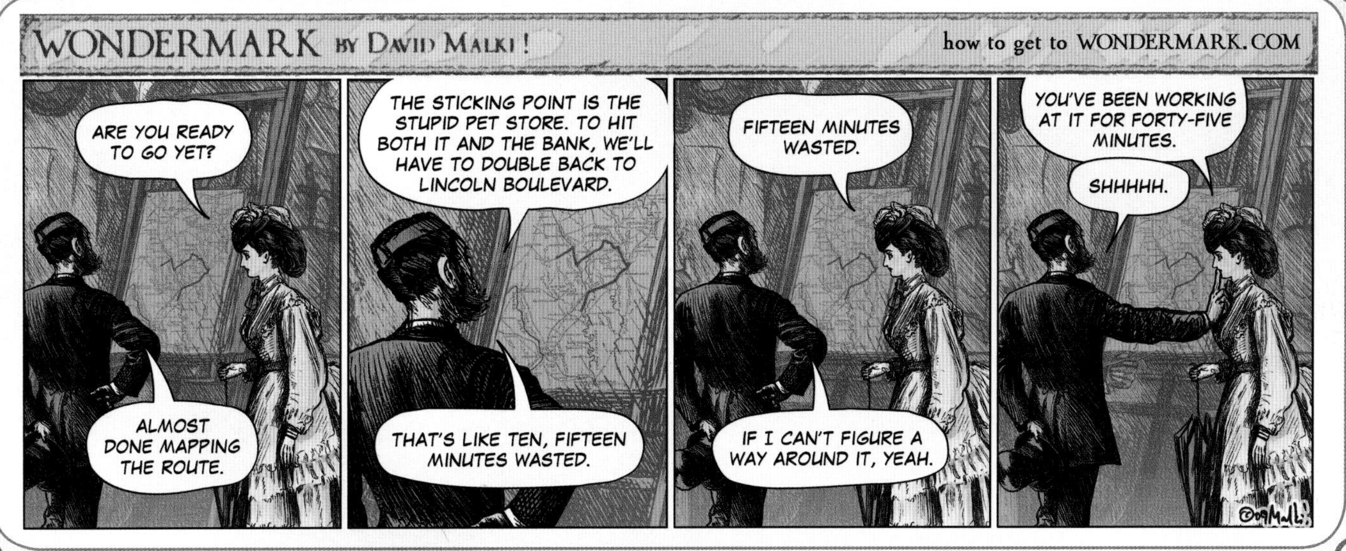

Let me do this.

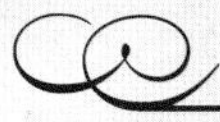

SOME STUPID PETS

Found At The Stupid Pet Store.

THIS Moron Puppy is remarkably stupid, even for a beast. All day it will batter itself gently against walls, table-legs, door-jambs, appliances, &c. Needless to say they do not yield to its pressure.—Besides the pup, we have seen an Imbecile Kitten. It produces a pathetic mewling which in no way approximates any language, even those of Europe. All its attempts to communicate are wholly unsuccessful.—No other animal can possibly be so stupid as this Blockhead Goldfish. It makes no sound at all, does not blink its eyes, has no job or evident means of financial support, and probably has never read so much as a pamphlet in all its life.—Similarly afflicted is this Dimwit Terrier. A few extra "dog years" have not given it any great advances in mind-power over the pup. The most clever thing we witnessed this dolt do all day was lick its berries. *Nice work, dog.*—A regular rat is no prize, but this Ignorant Rat is worse yet. Any American third grader can recite all 50 state capitals in an instant, but repeated interrogations of this rat yielded nothing for our interlocutor but the plague.—Another of this most sorry lot is the Turtle With Unpleasant Politics. When placed in a terrarium with electrified dolls of nonwhite races, it hides its head in its shell and refuses to emerge until the dolls have been removed.—But the absolute worst of all must be this Idiot Hamster. It just doesn't *do anything*.

IN WHICH AN OPPORTUNITY ESCAPES

WONDERMARK BY DAVID MALKI !

contribute at WONDERMARK.COM

THAT PART LOOKS PRETTY UNEVEN

©09 Malki!

YOUR *HEAD'S* UNEVEN, THAT'S WHAT I *SHOULD* HAVE SAID

Stampy, you want to race a train?

IN WHICH SPARKY CHANGES OWNERSHIP

WONDERMARK BY DAVID MALKI !
take on WONDERMARK.COM
CRIMINY, FOSTER! TOOK A BIT OF A TUMBLE THERE, EH?
IT'S FATAL, BARNES. FELL ON A JAGGED BRANCH. TASTING BARK IN MY THROAT EVEN NOW.
I'M DONE FOR, OLD CHUM.

BUT SPARKY'S STILL GOT A LIFE TO LIVE. TAKE HER AWAY FROM THIS BLASTED PLACE, WILL YOU? FIND HER SOME PASTURE TO ROAM...
WILL YOU DO IT, BARNES? WILL YOU ADOPT HER FOR ME? AND FEED HER, AND BRUSH HER, AND TEND TO HER COSTLY, MYRIAD AND UNUSUAL MEDICAL NEEDS?

WILL YOU HAND-MASH HER SPECIAL IMPORTED OATMEAL?
RUB HER DOWN EACH EVENING WITH A MITT HAND-KNIT FROM THE HAIRS OF HER OWN MANE?
TIVO ICE ROAD TRUCKERS FOR HER?
WILL YOU DRY HER TEARS WHEN LIGHTNING, TORNADOES AND SUN FRIGHTEN HER?
WILL YOU BUILD THE GIANT, CLIMATE-CONTROLLED BARN SHE'S ALWAYS WANTED FOR ALL THE STUFFED ANIMALS SHE HOPES TO COLLECT ON ALL THE TRAVELS YOU TAKE TOGETHER?

WILL YOU KNEAD HER GUMS THRICE DAILY?
WILL YOU HIRE ONLY THE BEST EQUESTRIAN-PILATES TRAINERS? AND WILL YOU DO THE EXERCISES WITH HER SO SHE DOESN'T GET SELF-CONSCIOUS? DESPITE THE FACT THAT THEY ARE DESIGNED FOR A HORSE'S BODY, NOT A MAN'S?

WILL YOU UNDERGO CATECHISM IN HER ANCIENT RELIGION?
WILL YOU TEACH YOUR CHILDREN THE SPOKEN LANGUAGE OF THE MIGHTY HORSE, SO SHE IS NOT THE LAST CONVERSATIONALIST OF HER STRANGE AND LILTING DIALECT?

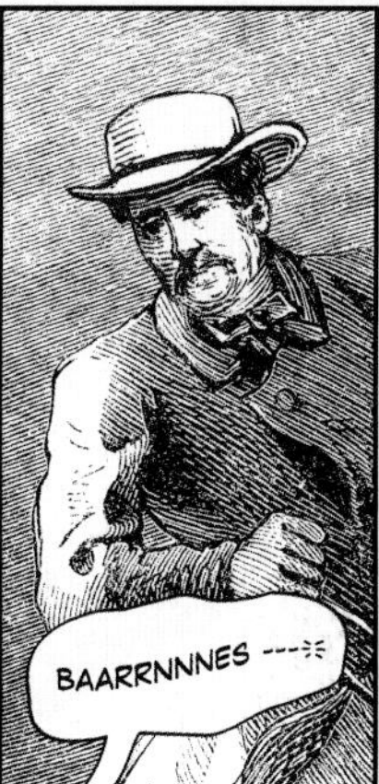

I can't believe I have to cook Sparky this massive dinner every night.

MUCH TO LOOK FORWARD TO

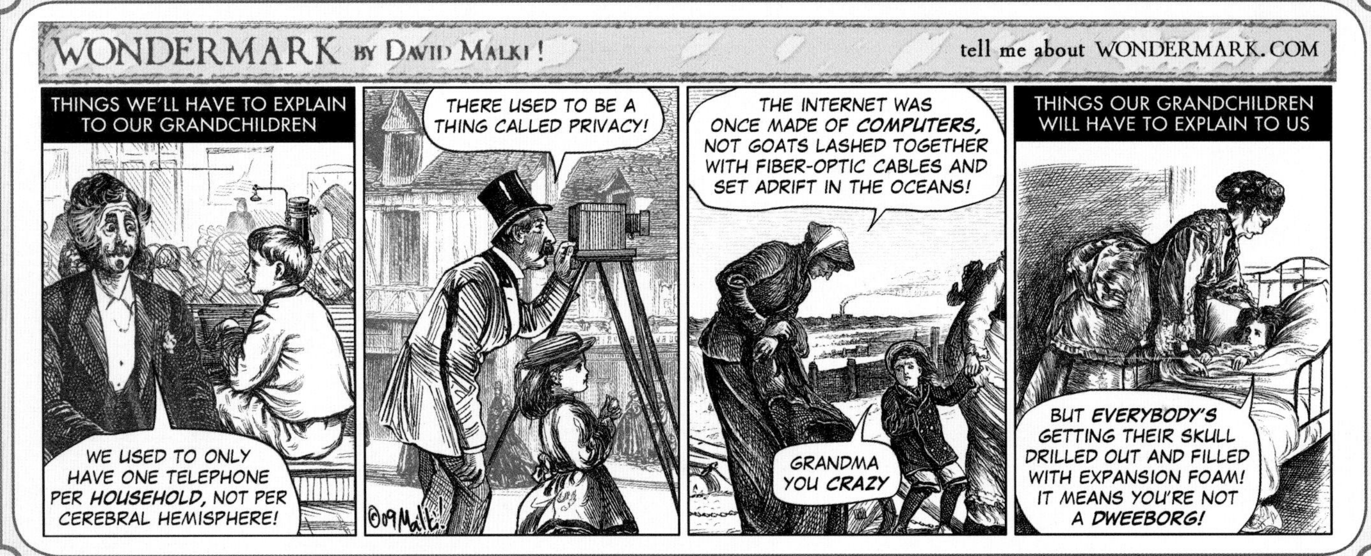

girls all having their sweet sixteen in the home depot parking lot

IN WHICH JAKE GETS A LEG UP

this is not really a business venture that scales

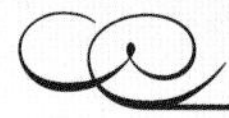

I don't know why Antonio thought that confession would make him LESS alluring.

A FALL FROM GRACE FOR NORBERT.

REGULAR READERS OF my column no doubt share my esteem for one of the greatest actors of our generation, Norbert the Elephant. His early work was charged with a pachydermite passion rarely seen in actors of his breeding, and even in small roles his unique charisma shone through like a strange, fascinating beacon in a fog-filled harbor, beckoning the eager viewer into a port bursting with rich import and crackling emotion. A turn of his trunk—or even the way the light danced on his tusks—spoke more in an instant than most actors today manage in an entire soliloquy.

SO IT PAINS ME TO ADMIT that Mr. the Elephant's latest roles have failed to meet the standard he himself set in his youth. A bold and pointed voice has seemingly been blunted by age and success; the Norbert of today scarcely resembles the angry young calf who first caught our attention as the clumsy but good-hearted villain in *In which an Interruption Occurs* (2003). In his latest, *In which Love is Unrequited,* his natural charm is lost beneath layers of special effects and a melodramatic script. Much as it pains me to hear Norbert's distinct baritone selling frozen peas in radio adverts of late, I prefer it to the one whispered line he is allowed in *Love.*

I HOPE SOME FUTURE DIRECTOR can recognize the great talent that lies fallow in Norbert at present. I hope Norbert himself can rediscover the powerful, singular trumpet that catapulted him to the top of the current era's greatest thespians. Until then, I am afraid I must be content to re-watch my copy of *In which Misfortune is Heralded* at home, and consign *In which Love is Unrequited* to a swift and thorough forgetting.

In the book you get all of Cynthia's internal monologue.

WONDERMARK BY DAVID MALKI !

it's raining WONDERMARK.COM

DO YOU STOCK PLUMBING SUPPLIES? I NEED SOME 5/8" BRASS FITTINGS.

OH, **NO!** THERE'S BEEN A ***CONTAMINATION SCARE*** ON BRASS FITTINGS!

EVERYTHING'S BEEN ***QUARANTINED!*** YOU DON'T HAVE ANY IN YOUR ***HOUSE,*** DO YOU?

CONTAMINATION— THAT DOESN'T REALLY MAKE—

BRASS HAS BEEN RECLASSIFIED A ***ZONE ALPHA DEADLY POISON!*** DON'T MOVE, YOU MIGHT BE INFECTED!

©09 Malki!

BRING IN THE DECONTAMINANT SCRUB!

THIS TASTES LIKE SPRAY GLUE

FSSSHHHTTT

LOOK OUT

HAHAHAHA!

YOU'VE

BEEN

STEAMPUNK'D!

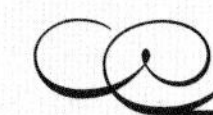

yo dawg I herd you like sprockets so I put sprockets in your sprockets
so you can sprocket while you sprocket

IN WHICH THE SPECIES IS BETTERED

Over the generations to come, some of us will die. Others of us will evolve into plastics.

IN WHICH WALTER TAKES A SUPPLEMENT

the more you struggle the sweeter it gets

It wasn't

A Thrilling Excerpt From

"JUSTICE TO THE LEFT!"

"IT'S THAT BLASTED meddler! Flatten 'im, lads!" MacDougal called to the men in overalls, raising his own revolver. Three quick shots cracked the air—*Tak! Tak! Tak!* But Dawson simply cocked his head, as if listening. MacDougal never even saw the bullets hit—but the whines of ricochets laid three of his strikers flat.

"Blast that bullet-proof ear!" MacDougal shouted again. "Surround 'im, boys! He can't point that thing at all of us at once!" Urged by his words, the young factory workers clutched their pistols, circling around the spot where Dawson had disappeared into the clouds of steam.

"We can end this now if you'll simply agree to work a full day for the same pay as everyone else," came the disembodied voice of the crime-fighter, piercing through the haze like an arrow. Nervous hands trembled on the grips of guns, palms slick with rank criminal sweat. "It's not too late. We can forget all of this, before more of you get hurt."

"We'd rather die!" MacDougal snarled, his red hair flying before his eyes like a tartan battle-flag. *Tak! Tak! Tak!* The revolver spat again, but again Dawson preternaturally anticipated their flight. The caroms echoed across the factory floor, punctuated only by the sounds of the strikers' pierced bodies hitting the cement.

"Sounds like you're out of bullets," Dawson smiled. MacDougal threw the gun at the shadowy figure.

"I still got fists, you rat!"

Dawson burst from the fog, looming tall above the sniveling goon. "If you think you can hit me anywhere besides the ear," he said, gently flexing his neck back and forth—*crack! crack!*—MacDougal sweating more with each pop—"well, you can just go ahead and try."

—from *Justice to the Left! Sherman Dawson Vs. The Union* (1908)

WONDERMARK BY DAVID MALKI !
fit just right at WONDERMARK.COM
GAAHH! I HATE PARKING!
NO PARKING
RESIDENTIAL PERMIT EXCEPTED
COMMERCIAL PERMIT EXCEPTED
DIPLOMATIC PERMIT EXCEPTED
DISABLED PLACARD EXCEPTED
VIGILANTE HERO PLACARD EXCEPTED
NO PARKING
DURING STREET CLEANING
MONDAY 5AM-11PM
TUESDAY 5AM-11PM
WEDNESDAY 5AM-11PM
THURSDAY 5AM-11PM
FRIDAY 5AM-11PM
SATURDAY 5AM-11PM
SUNDAY 5AM-11PM
THE STREET IS REALLY DIRTY OKAY
NO PARKING
EVERYONE EXCEPT GUYS WITH MOUSTACHES EXCEPTED
GAAHHH!!
HOW WOULD THEY EVEN KNOW?
HEY, MIKE? REMEMBER THE TIME I SAVED YOU FROM THAT SNAKEBITE?
...I NEED A FAVOR.

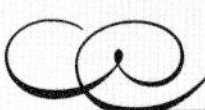

This is sufficient to qualify for the Vigilante Hero placard.

IN WHICH A TALE IS RECOUNTED FOR POSTERITY

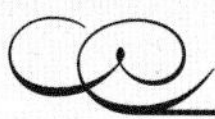

The final published account of the carrots-in-the-icebox incident reads like Rashomon.

BACK WHEN ALL SEEMED BRIGHT

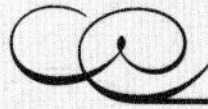

"If he would just stop inventing things he may yet grow up to be successful."

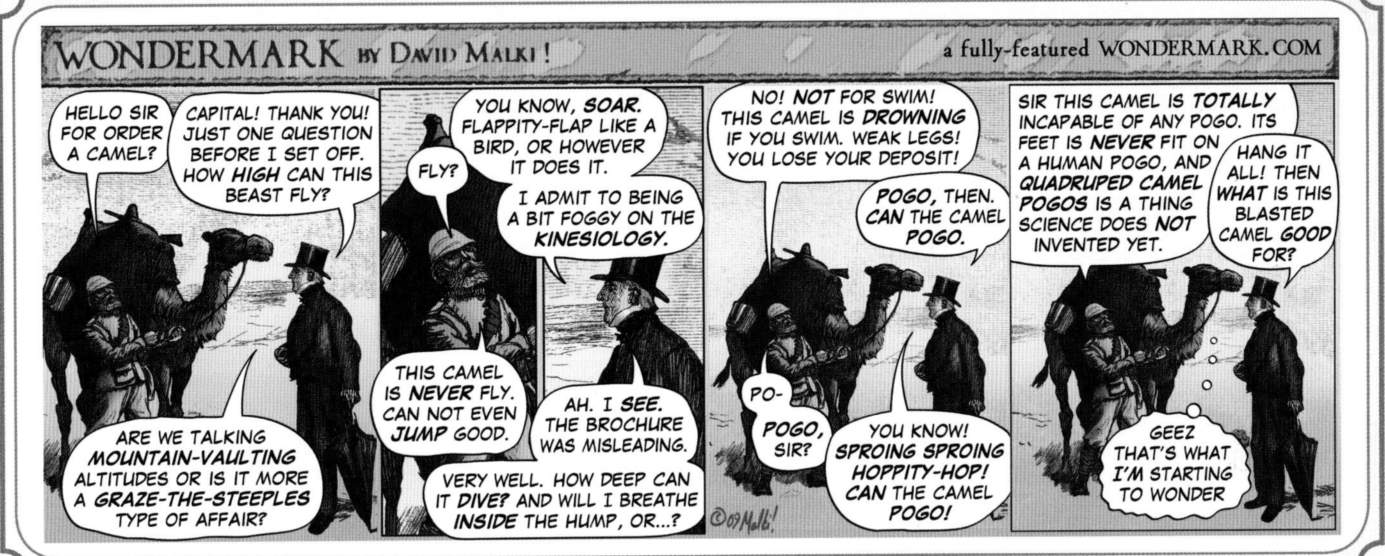

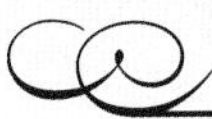

We put temporary authorization on your credit card in case camel comes back drowned

AA Best Camel Rental Ltd.

★★☆☆☆ 48 reviews

Category: Animal Leasing

24 E. Dusty Wastes
Neighborhood: Empty Quarter

27 reviews in English

★☆☆☆☆ 10/6/09

What a rip off…I came with my family based on a Groupon we got for 12 hours' free space flight. Not only can the camels not hold more than 2 people, they also apparently CANNOT leave Earth's atmosphere. The guy was apologetic but CLEARLY had not seen the ad himself. Seemed frustrated like he's had to deal with this all day…Anyway he gave us half off and we spent a very bumpy 1/2 hour walking in a circle around the city well before my youngest got sick and we called it a day. VERY disappointed and a reminder to check the BBB before buying a Groupon!

Was this review …? Useful • (2) Funny • Cool •

★☆☆☆☆ 9/18/09

If I could give zero stars I would! I used to pass by this place every day and finally decided to give them a try. I got a Valpak coupon in the mail for "free upgrade to Ghost Camel which can" -- this is verbatim -- "take you on a spectral tour of the realm of the beyond." Well my boyfriend's b-day was coming up and he's into Ghost Rider so I thought what the heck. DO NOT pay for the upgrade, it's just a ratty sheet on top of a regular camel!! The clerk was visibly exasperated when I showed him the coupon and I think he came up with the sheet thing just so I wouldn't walk out. NOT recommended.

Was this review …? Useful • Funny • (1) Cool •

★★★☆☆ 7/20/09

Three stars for a mixed experience…The camels are dirty and no fun, but there's a 16-year-old kid there who apparently writes all the ads and promotions without telling his dad. He's got a thousand-yard stare and, when I asked about the "race car package" I got an email about, he just said "I put it out there just in case it comes true." I felt melancholy for the rest of the day. In fact, it's been a week and that look in his eyes is still haunting me. That's worth three stars I think.

Was this review …? Useful • Funny • Cool • (4)

IN WHICH A STUDY IS STYMIED

WONDERMARK BY DAVID MALKI !

take note of WONDERMARK.COM

ALL RIGHT, LET'S SEE HOW YOU TASTE.

YOU BEEN EATING SOME PRETTY WEIRD STUFF LATELY.

YOU ON THAT BRONZE AGE DIET?

NAH, I'M PART OF A SURVEY GROUP. BUNCH OF SCIENTISTS TRACK WHAT I EAT FOR A COUPLE YEARS.

THEN THEY PUT ALL THE DATA TOGETHER AND SAY "TEN PERCENT OF THE COFFEE DRINKERS CONTRACTED CANCER" OR WHATEVER.

TRYING TO FIND WHAT CONTRIBUTES TO ILLNESSES.

YEAH. BUT I COULDN'T TAKE IT.

EVERY TIME I HAD A SNICKERS I'D THINK, "IS THIS IT? IS THIS THE ONE THAT GIVES ME LEUKEMIA?"

SO I GOT A ***NEW*** IDEA. I'M PLANNING TO DIE OF SOME SUPER-RARE DISEASE – LIKE, ***SO*** RARE THEY ***NAME*** IT AFTER ME.

AND I'M ***ALSO*** GONNA EAT THE STUPIDEST STUFF I CAN FIND.

THAT WAY I LEAVE THE SCIENTISTS SCRATCHING THEIR HEADS – "WELL, HE ATE TWENTY POUNDS OF CUCUMBERS EVERY DAY FOR TEN YEARS, THEN DIED OF THIS PREVIOUSLY UNKNOWN LIVER DISEASE."

EAT ***THAT,*** SCIENTISTS!

METAPHORICALLY, OF COURSE.

WELL, IT'S GOOD TO HAVE GOALS!

TEN YEARS LATER

YOU HAVE TERMINAL PROSTATE CANCER.

BOO-RRRING

©09 Malki !

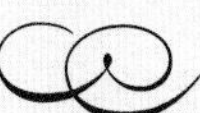

Supposedly the cucumber is the only food that contains every necessary nutrient, albeit only in trace amounts for some. So if you're going to restrict yourself to a single food, twenty pounds of cucumbers is a reasonably smart choice.

IN WHICH A CAREER TAKES A TURN

Anna Wintour templed her perfect fingers. "Now," she hissed, "we wait."

IN WHICH A TOOL IS IMPROVED

To be fair, most of his projects don't get quite this advanced.

INUTILITY OF A JINGLE

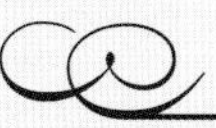

I guarantee I will never buy a car from the Cerritos Auto Center but boy can I give you some snappy directions to it.

IN WHICH FULL PRICE IS BEGRUDGINGLY PAID

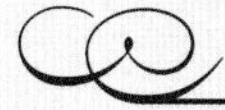

I hear the rival bar across the street offers a CRAZY discount if you stand in front of their door shouting at passersby with a megaphone.

OLD-COUNTRY GRANDPARENTS

"Old country" is defined as "anyplace where there is a goat in the kitchen"

IN WHICH SUSIE DOES NOT LEARN

Will Susie become a ward of the state? OR OF THE PIRANHAMOOSE?

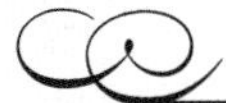

THE PREVALENCE OF INTERNAL LOGIC

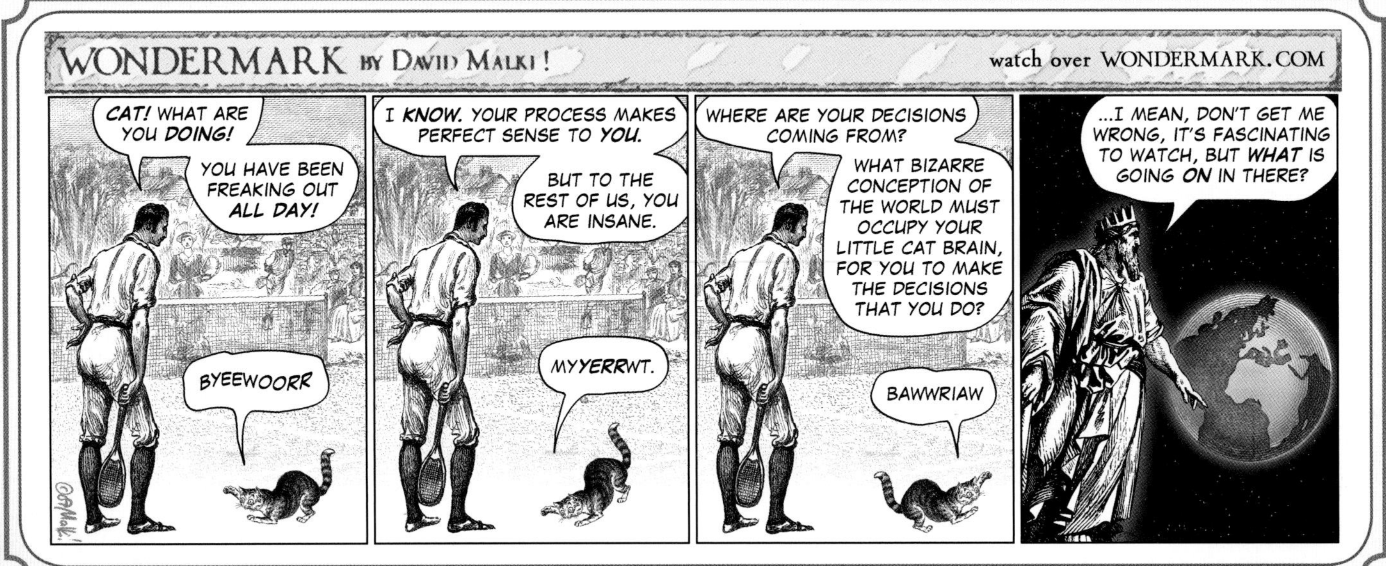

all together now: "BWYAAIOOOW"

IN WHICH A DIVERSION FAILS TO IMPRESS

haha he wrote *The Secret* right

IN WHICH IT'S HARD TO TELL

I can't WAIT to hear what you half-remember the confusing details of next.

THE MASTERS OF TEA

We amass information mainly to keep it from our competitors.

WONDERMARK BY DAVID MALKI !
send yourself to WONDERMARK.COM
...IT WAS THOUGHT THE FICTION OF A COURT-MARTIAL WOULD PREVENT YOU FROM TOO SOON REGAINING CONTROL OF YOUR VESSEL.
CAPTAIN PIKE IS WELCOME TO SPEND THE REST OF HIS LIFE WITH US, UNFETTERED BY HIS PHYSICAL BODY.
THE DECISION IS YOURS. AND HIS.
CHRIS...
DO YOU WANT TO GO THERE?
SEE HIM OFF.
THANK YOU, SIR. FOR BOTH OF US.
©09 Malki !

Now Commences A Section Of

FAILED AND GUEST COMICS.

ON THE NEXT SEVERAL pages you will find a series of work-in-progress comics that I have elected to abandon. The reasons for this are myriad and usually involve blackmail, but for the sake of this collection we shall assume they were simply *not good enough*. In most cases these failed comics take the form of scripts that were never developed into finished comic format, and so they appear here either visually incomplete *or* rendered in our new SilhouetteVision™ technique, which permits the script to be read and understood but which does not require the level of effort on my part that completing a full comic would. If these were worth turning into full comics, *they would have been.*

Following the failed comics, you will find a pastiche comic I created in the style of artist Tony Millionaire, as well as a number of guest comics created by other artists in the style of Wondermark. I am sad to report that I have no knowledge of any pastiches Tony Millionaire has created in the style of any of the guest artists, and thus the circle remains imcomplete. That is why they are all grouped here, with the *failures.*

FAILURE #1

There's a funny idea here, but I could never quite get this to look the way I wanted.

FAILURE #2

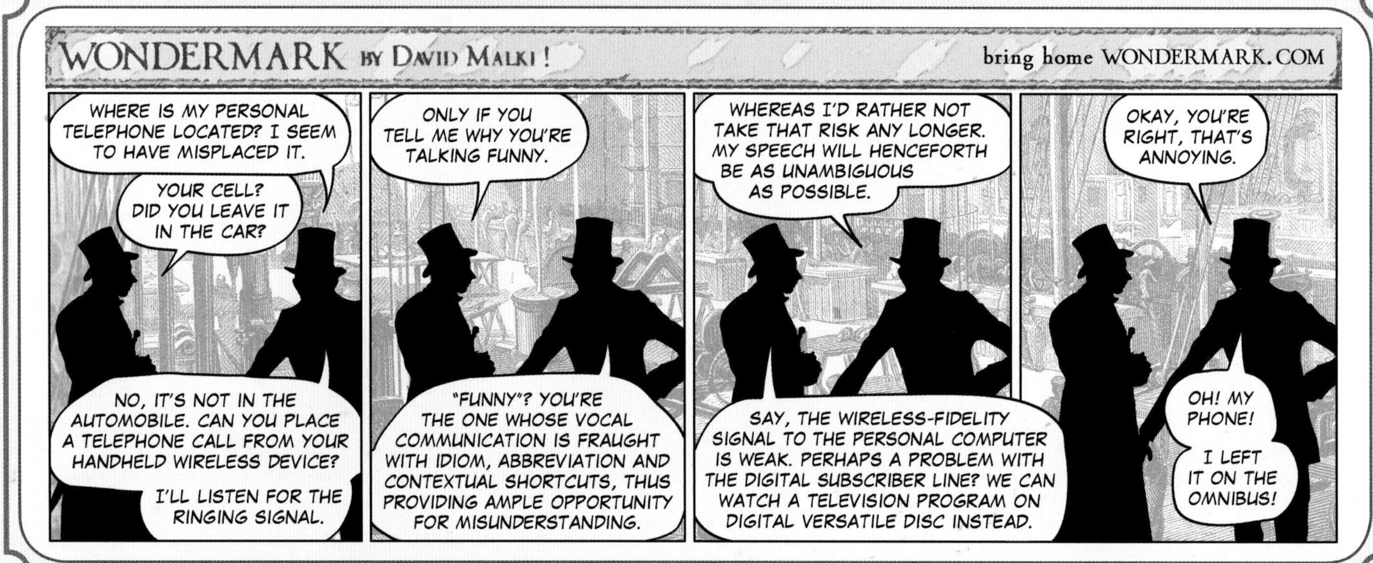

Full disclosure: this setup was just a contrivance to get to use the word "omnibus" (in the public-transit sense of the word)

FAILURE #3

Any draft of anything that sits on a hard drive, unfinished, for over five years (like this comic) should probably just be thrown away.

FAILURE #4

This would work as one episode of a longer story, or if we knew who the characters were. One limitation of the gag-a-day format is that a joke like this lacks the nuance that recurring characters would bring to it.

FAILURE #5

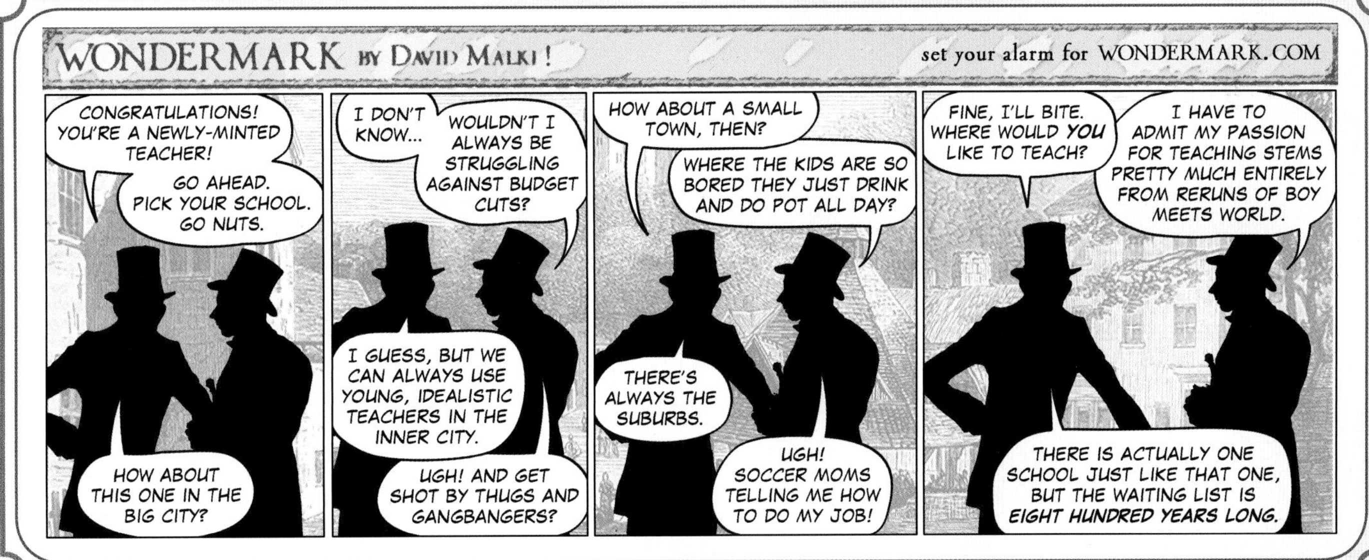

You can tell I'm a square because I use the phrase "do pot"

FAILURE #6

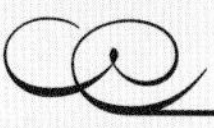

This feels like a first- or second-year Wondermark strip to me.

FAILURE #7

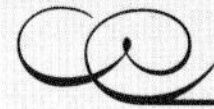

I typically don't curse in the strip, but sometimes only certain words can communicate the desired effect.

FAILURE #8

I forget why I thought this one would be too difficult to finish.

FAILURE #9

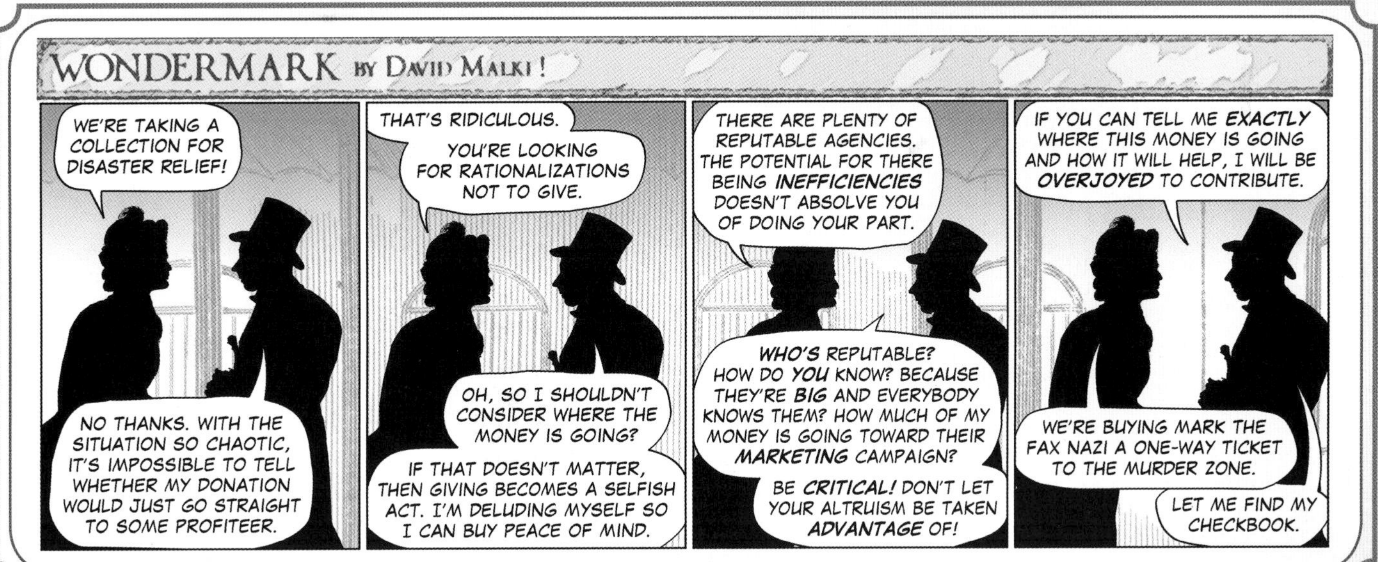

I worried this was too contrived. Do people who work in offices really say things like "Mark the Fax Nazi"?

IN WHICH AN CROW DRINKS OFF-PANEL

MAALKIES!
WHOA-OA!
HOLD'ER STEADY!
WITH APOLOGIES + RESPECT TO TONY MILLIONAIRE
THERE'S NOTHIN' I CAN DO! SOMETHIN'S FOULING UP MY CONTROLS!
THAT ROTTEN MAALKI! IS UP TO NO GOOD!
MY BEARD'S IN THE SPROCKETS AGAIN
THE DAY I MET TONY MILLIONAIRE
HERE IS A SAMPLE OF "WONDERMARK"!
HMMMM
WHAT IS THIS GARBAGE

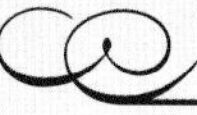

To be fair, I don't know that he was thinking that EXACTLY.

GUEST COMIC BY RANDALL MUNROE

The things I have seen, Bartleby! A man named Goat See has rediscovered Leonardo's "Tunnel of Knowledge" festival trick.

GUEST COMIC BY KC GREEN

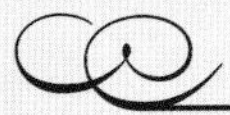

I happen to have his card right here! [UNPRINTABLE GESTURE]

GUEST COMIC BY ANGELA MELICK

WONDERMARK BY DAVID MALKI ! GUEST STRIP BY JAM WASTEDTALENT.CA Get Satisfaction at WONDERMARK.COM

HEY, MAN! HOW MUCH FOR A HOT DOG??
FOUR DOLLA'
MAAAAAAAN!
HEY, MAN! HOW MUCH FOR A PRETZEL??
TWO FIDDY.
MAAAAAAAN!
OH GOD... SO HUNGRY!
I NEED SOMETHING... ANYTHING!
TIC-TAC...
STICK O' GUM...
ICE-COLD SODA...
HEY LADY, HOW MUCH FOR THAT BABY??
ONE DOLLA'
AW-RIIIIIGHT!

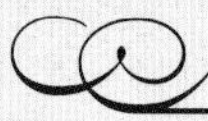

"Ketchup, five dolla." *MAAAAANNNN*

If some of the details of this comic seem unusual or overly-specific, it is because it is inspired by a true story. Suffice it to say that I need never return to Baltimore.

For larger versions of Angela's drawings, see: jammyness.livejournal.com/257593.html

GUEST COMIC BY JOHN KEOGH

WONDERMARK BY JOHN KEOGH : LUCID-TV.COM at WONDERMARK.COM

Beardless

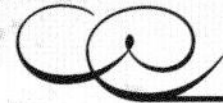

Mommy! Hold me in your beard, and comfort me.

AT LEFT.

THIS COMIC was created as part of the "Unshelved Book Club," a weekly series of illustrated book reviews. *The Confessions of Max Tivoli* (Farrar, Straus and Giroux, 2004) is a marvelous book that unfortunately shares a premise with the much more well-known *Benjamin Button* movie that followed a few years later. However, I enjoyed *Max Tivoli* far more and urge interested parties to seek out a copy.

WWW.UNSHELVED.COM/BOOKCLUB

AT RIGHT.

THE STORY on the following pages was commissioned by Dark Horse Comics, and first saw print in the anthology *MySpace Dark Horse Presents* #5 (2010). It was colored by Marcus Parcus.

ON PAGE 101.

THE PIRANHAMOOSE children's tale was found who-knows-where, and unearthed and sent to me by Sharon Bryan. It features illustrations by Phil McAndrew (1840-1912).

"The Gax of Life" A WONDERMARK TALE BY David Malki !

THIS PLANET'S INHABITANTS REACT STRANGELY TO MY USUAL ULTRASONIC MATING SCREECH. EVERY TIME I TRY IT, IT ONLY SEEMS TO ATTRACT **DOGS.**
I'M NOT SURE WHAT I'M DOING WRONG.
WELL, GAX, IT'S BECAUSE HUMAN WOMEN DON'T EVEN HAVE THE RIGHT ORGANS TO **HEAR** GAXIAN ULTRASONIC MATING CALLS!

OH, **NO,** RICK. I ASSURE YOU THEY **DO.**

HOW... HOW DO YOU KNOW?

BUT YOU SEE? **DOGS.**

WITH ALL DUE RESPECT TO THE LOVELY YOUNG LADY CURRENTLY MASSAGING MY TAIL...
THIS IS NOT THE ONE I WANT.
HOW DO I GET THE ONE I *WANT?*
I—
I WAS JUST EATING MY LUNCH WHEN ALL OF A SUDDEN MY FEET STARTED MOVING

LISTEN, GAX. I'M GLAD YOU CAME TO ME WITH THIS.
IT'S AN IMPORTANT STEP IN ONE'S LIFE WHEN YOU STOP SIMPLY TAKING WHOMEVER IS DRAWN IN BY YOUR HORRIFIC SQUEAL AND START FOLLOWING YOUR HEART.
YOU **DO** HAVE A HEART, RIGHT? OR SOME EQUIVALENT ORGAN?

I HAVE A COLLECTION OF HUMAN HEARTS THAT I KEEP AS TROPHIES FROM PAST ENCOUNTERS WITH YOUR SOFT KIND
ALL RIGHT. SO YOU KNOW WHAT I MEAN.

NOW LOOK. GIRLS LIKE IT WHEN YOU'RE ***SWEET*** AND ***ROMANTIC.***
IS THERE A ***SPECIFIC*** GIRL THAT YOU LIKE?

OUR RECEPTIONIST AT WORK.
DEBBIE.
PERFECT! WHAT'S SHE LIKE?
OH, RICK. SHE IS LIKE A GAXIAN ANGEL. EXCEPT WITHOUT THE HORNS.

THE GENTLE CURVE OF HER EAR IS LIKE THE BUTTERY SHELL OF A MEAT-SNAIL. IT IS SO HARD EACH MORNING TO STOP FROM LEANING OVER THE DESK AND TAKING A LICK.

HER SKIN IS SQUISHY AND WOULD YIELD TANTALIZINGLY TO THE CLAW.

AND HER RIBS! OH, HER RIBS ARE BEYOND CAPACIOUS ENOUGH TO BEAR A GIANT BROOD OF GAXIAN EGG-CLOTS.

YEAH, I LIKE A LITTLE SOMETHIN' UP FRONT TOO. OKAY, SO WHY NOT BRING HER SOME FLOWERS? THAT RECEPTION DESK IS PROBABLY PRETTY DRAB.
FLOWERS? OH, I THINK I SEE THE LOGIC!
ANY WOMAN WHO REACTS POSITIVELY TO A SUDDEN OFFERING OF SEVERED PLANT GENITALS IS LIKELY TO RESPOND EQUALLY WELL TO A SUBSEQUENT AND IMMEDIATE OFFERING OF MY OWN

NO! GAX
PEOPLE WHO DO THAT GET PUT ON LISTS
THEY CAN NEVER LIVE NEAR A SCHOOL
I CAN SEE IT NOW...
FIRST I PRESENT DEBBIE WITH THE PLANT GENITALS, TO GET HER WARM TO THE IDEA OF MY GENITALS.
THEN I ALLOW MY GENITALS TO UNLEASH THEIR OWN ULTRASONIC SQUEAL! OF COURSE!
THAT WAS THE MISSING COMPONENT! IT'S THE GENITAL SQUEAL! OH, RICK, I CAN'T THANK YOU ENOUGH!

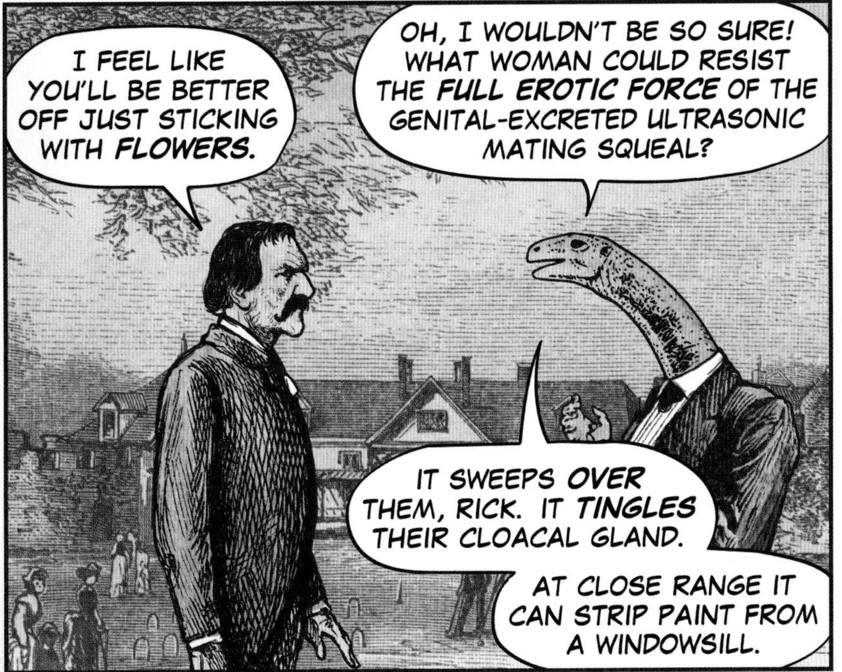

I SEE.
UNFORTUNATELY THAT IS IMPOSSIBLE, AS MY CARAPACE HAS ALREADY FUSED.
IN MY SPECIES IT HAPPENS EARLY.

DO YOU THINK I'M TOO OLD TO FIND TRUE LOVE, RICK?

NO! LOOK, ALL YOU HAVE TO DO IS TAKE DEBBIE ON A NICE DATE.
HAVE SOME FUN! SHOW HER A LITTLE OF YOURSELF.
AH! OF COURSE. SO I DISPLAY MY GENITALS ON THE DATE!
I WOULD LIKE TO MAKE THE GENITAL-DATE TODAY, IF THAT IS POSSIBLE

TAKE IT ONE STEP AT A TIME. MAYBE TRY A BACKRUB? SEE WHERE IT GOES FROM THERE.
CAPITAL! MY SPECIES IS EXCELLENT AT BACKRUBS. IN FACT, WE HAVE AN ORGAN DESIGNED SPECIFICALLY FOR IT!

IS IT YOUR GENITALS?
YES.

GAX. SPEAKING AS A FRIEND.
YOU CANNOT JUST SHOW THIS WOMAN YOUR GENITALS. IT'S NOT HOW HUMANS BEHAVE.
BUT WHY NOT? IN GAXIAN CULTURE, SHOWING ONE'S GENITALS TO A ROMANTIC PARTNER IS THE ULTIMATE SIGN OF AFFECTION AND TRUST!

AND LOOK. I UNDERSTAND THAT HUMANS DO SOME VERY STRANGE THINGS. LIKE ALL SPECIES EXCEPT THE COCKROACHES, YOU HAVE HAD A COMPLICATED AND CAPRICIOUS EVOLUTION.
FOR EXAMPLE, YOU DO NOT DEVOUR YOUR MOTHERS AT THE INSTANT OF YOUR BIRTH. THIS I WILL NEVER UNDERSTAND.
I HAVE SHOUTED AT BABIES, PHYSICALLY SHOUTED AT THEM, TRYING TO ACTIVATE A MATRIVOROUS INSTINCT I WAS SURE WAS BURIED IN THERE. NOTHING.
IT'S A WONDER YOU PEOPLE SURVIVE AS YOU DO, ALL THOSE MOTHERS AND GRANDMOTHERS OUT THERE, WALKING AROUND UN-DEVOURED FOR PROTEIN.

UGH, CAN THIS PLEASE NOT TURN INTO ANOTHER DEBATE ABOUT THE MERITS OF THE GAXIAN FAMILY STRUCTURE.
I DO NOT NEED TO FIGHT MY SIBLINGS FOR THE RIGHT TO SUCK THE MARROW FROM MY FATHER'S BONES.
BUT RICK! HOW THEN ARE YOU TO ABSORB HIS GARAX'IR, HIS BLESSED PATRIARCHAL BONE-VENOM?
I ASK EVERY HUMAN I MEET THIS QUESTION! NOBODY HAS A GOOD ANSWER!
BUT BACK TO GENITALS

OF ALL SPECIES, I'D IMAGINE YOU GUYS WOULD TREAT GENITAL DISPLAY AS SACRED!
OBVIOUSLY IT'S DIFFERENT IF YOU'RE THE EYRAH AND YOUR GENITALS ARE THE SIZE OF MOUNTAINS, OR IF YOU'RE THE P'TARR AND YOUR GENITALS GLOW IN THE DARK.
AND ARE THE SIZE OF MOUNTAINS.
OR, YOU KNOW, EVEN IF YOU'RE THE BLARNAZZ AND YOU REQUIRE FIFTEEN GENDERS TO REPRODUCE. YOU GOTTA BE WAVING THOSE THINGS AROUND ALL DAY LONG JUST TO GET A BIG ENOUGH PARTY GOING.

YOU MADE ALL THOSE THINGS UP, DIDN'T YOU?
ANYWAY MY POINT IS

IS GENITAL-DISPLAY NOT PRIZED AMONG YOUR KIND? IS IT NOT A COMPLIMENT TO BE GIFTED WITH A BOUT OF PEACOCKING?
OR AS WE CALL IT, HAVING NO PEACOCKS ON GAX, "SXZK-COCKING"
NO, NO. SEE, IT IS A SIGN OF AFFECTION, BUT...YOU CAN'T JUST START OUT WITH THAT. YOU GOT TO SHIFT INTO THAT GEAR ONCE YOU GET GOING A LITTLE.

START SLOW. YOU SEE WHAT I'M SAYING?
YOU'RE BACK TO THE FLOWERS.
SURE. THAT CAN BE STEP ONE. THEN YOU MOVE ON TO STEP TWO, AND THEN STEP THREE AND SO ON. AND AT STEP, LIKE, FIFTY— YOU CAN SHOW YOUR GENITALS.

THERE ARE FORTY-NINE STEPS OF FLOWERS?
THIS IS ALL TOO MUCH TO LEARN! ARE THESE ALL DIFFERENT TYPES OF FLOWERS OVER TIME? I TRUST THAT THEY PROGRESSIVELY BUILD TO THE GREAT GENITAL REVEAL?
NO! GAX —
YOU'RE BEING WILLFULLY IGNORANT. STOP IT.
YOU KNOW THAT'S NOT WHAT I MEANT.

DO I, RICK? DO YOU KNOW ME SO WELL THAT YOU KNOW EVERYTHING THAT I DO AND DO NOT UNDERSTAND?
UH — DO — DO I KNOW THAT YOU KNOW THAT — WAIT HOLD ON

I WAS BORN FROM AN EGG, RICK. I ATE MY MOTHER AND THEN I WENT TO SCHOOL IN A VOLCANO.
I WAS FROZEN IN HYPERSPACE FOR FIFTY THOUSAND YEARS AND WHEN I FINALLY WOKE UP, I WAS AT THE BOTTOM OF SOME EARTH OCEAN.

I MAY BE THE LAST OF MY SPECIES IN THE UNIVERSE. I HAVE PAINSTAKINGLY LEARNED YOUR STUPID LANGUAGE AND TAKEN A STUPID JOB AT A STUPID AD AGENCY SO I CAN BUY YOUR STUPID FOOD SO I DO NOT DIE.
BUT I DO NOT LIKE IT.

EVERYTHING YOU PEOPLE DO IS NONSENSE TO ME. WATCH TELEVISION? STUPID. EAT PLANTS? STUPID. HIDE YOUR GENITALS? STUPID.
BUT I AM HERE NOW. I HAVE NO CHOICE BUT TO LIVE HERE. SO I AM TRYING MY GAX-DANG BEST TO LEARN, AND FIT IN, AND DO THINGS RIGHT, AND MAKE FRIENDS.

AND MAYBE EVEN FIND SOMEONE WHO WILL, SOMEDAY, POSSIBLY, AGAINST ALL ASTRONOMICAL ODDS, CHOOSE TO DISPLAY THEIR GENITALS TO ME. IS THAT OKAY, RICK?
YOU PEOPLE WON'T LET ME RELIEVE MY ACID DUCTS IN PUBLIC. YOU WON'T LET ME TEACH YOUR BABIES ANYTHING USEFUL. BUT CAN I AT LEAST HAVE THIS? CAN I AT LEAST TRY FOR A LITTLE SLIVER OF HAPPINESS?

I AM TRYING, RICK.
I'M SORRY. GEEZ. I DIDN'T REALIZE.

IT'S JUST...
WELL, NEVER MIND. SO, THE FLOWERS...
WAIT, NO. JUST WHAT?

IT'S NOTHING.
NO, YOU WERE GOING TO SAY SOMETHING. TELL ME WHAT YOU WERE GOING TO SAY.

SOMETIMES...
JUST SOMETIMES, I THINK YOU LIKE TO PLAY THE "OH I'M JUST A BEFUDDLED ALIEN" CARD A LITTLE TOO OFTEN.
I MEAN, YOU'VE BEEN HERE HOW LONG? YOU COULD GET THIS STUFF. IT'S NOT THAT COMPLICATED.
THAT'S WHAT IMMIGRANTS DO. THEY ASSIMILATE.
BUT YOU DON'T. YOU JUST GET MAD.

YOU SEE? THIS!
THIS IS WHAT I'M TALKING ABOUT RIGHT HERE!

WE DON'T REGENERATE THESE!
YOU DON'T? OH, SHOOT, MAN, MY BAD.

I WILL **NEVER** UNDERSTAND HUMANS

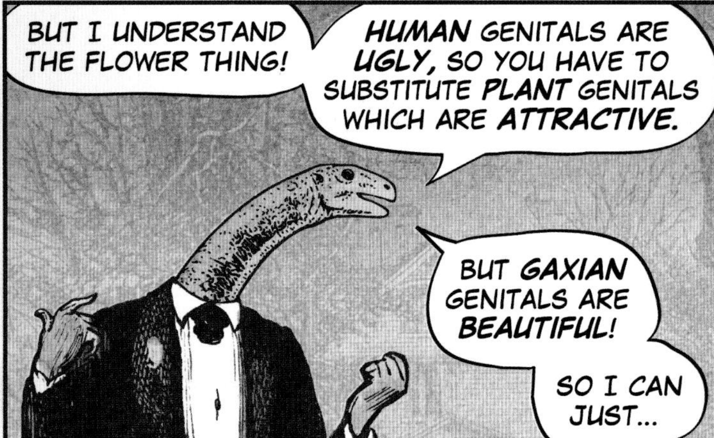
BUT I UNDERSTAND THE FLOWER THING!
HUMAN GENITALS ARE **UGLY,** SO YOU HAVE TO SUBSTITUTE **PLANT** GENITALS WHICH ARE **ATTRACTIVE.**
BUT **GAXIAN** GENITALS ARE **BEAUTIFUL!**
SO I CAN JUST...

DEBBIE DO YOU WANT TO GO ON A DATE
OH MY GOODNESS GAX I THOUGHT YOU'D NEVER ASK

The Awesome Piranhamoose

AN INSTRUCTIVE TALE FOR CHILDREN

by

Charlene Ludwig

When you and your father
go down to the zoo
Beware of the critters
who'd like to eat you

The giraffes are okay,
as they only eat leaves
But the lions will eat
just whatever they please

And beware of the bear
with the ill-fitting hat,
For many a child
has been eaten by that

Though the hat may seem
jaunty on top of his head
The killer who wears it
will make you quite dead

But now, oh my children,
do not act the goose
Stay away from the cage
of the Piranhamoose

For this awesome creature's
a killing machine
Its teeth are so sharp
and its antlers so keen

It will gore you and eat you
and spit out your bones
Oh, my dears, leave the
Piranhamoose well alone!

The hunters who
captured it long, long ago,
In the wild Yukon jungles,
regretted it so

For it ate all their children, and some of their wives
And no one goes near it for fear of their lives

My dears, I can see that wild look in your eye
You so want to touch it – you so want to try

But please, heed your mother
and stay far away
And do not jump over
the barrier today

Your father is ready,
now promise me, do
You won't touch that Piranhamoose,
now will you?

ASK  GAX.

Our Syndicated Advice Column.

DEAR GAX: I work in an office with five other people. One of my co-workers is a compulsive coffee drinker. The rest of us drink a moderate amount.

The office rule is that whoever drinks the last cup must make more. Yet often the coffee-hound drinks most of the pot, leaving half a cup or so for the next person, who must inevitably make a new pot despite not drinking much of the previous one. Shouldn't the person who drinks the most coffee shoulder most of the burden of making more? How can we enforce this in the office?

—FORCIBLY DECAFFEINATED

DEAR FORCIBLY: Your office cannot function at peak efficiency if you are constantly being bothered by this petty coffee squabbling. Have you tried asking the coffee-fiend nicely to make more pots more often, in the selfless interest of interoffice tranquility? Some individuals must always sacrifice for the good of the hive. My guess from the tone of your letter, however, is that you have not even bothered to address your concern with this person directly. You write me passive-aggressively, perhaps hoping that the coffee-drinker will see his letter here and wordlessly correct his behavior, sparing both of you the awkwardness of a confrontation. This is unlikely to work, but if the aim is not to rectify the problem but rather to satisfy your urge to have "done something about" the problem, congratulations. You are quite the hero.

If this coffee thing is bothering you so much, simply follow the person to his car, wait until he closes the door (with the windows rolled up), place a 4-mil solar bomb against the driver's window and flash-heat the interior of the car to five million degrees. It will appear as if he died from sunstroke and you will be in the clear. Do not write me when you then have to deal with this man's extra workload, however. Every decisive action changes the game board.

—Gax, challengingly

DEAR GAX: My husband is a kind and supportive soul, with one exception. Whenever I try to fix something around the house, he gets in my way, insisting that I'm doing it wrong and that he be the one to make any repairs. But he never has the time, and it's not like he's Bob Vila, either: I'm just as handy as he is. And if he finds that I've done something while he's gone, he'll nitpick it to death and often keep tinkering with it himself until it's "perfect." How can I get out of this marriage?

—NEEDS REPAIR

Dear Needs,

When home life becomes so tranquil that minor quarrels are elevated into insurmountable hurdles, truly you live a charmed life. When I was growing up, I had to battle five thousand swarming siblings to suck tiny drops of spilled blood from scalding rocks. It was my only source of nourishment throughout my entire elementary-school career. If someone stopped attempting to claw my eyes out long enough to offer to fix my sink, *even if he never did it* I would still consider this person heart-bonded to me for life. It is an expression of compassion that you are reading as contempt, and for that you should be made to run the Graxfian Path. If you reach Spine Rock before dying of metabolic disease you will be able to choose a new mate from the egg-broods there.

If you choose not to do this, you should instead learn how to fix the sink such that when he attempts to continue tinkering, he is scalded with boiling wastewater. If you can manage to assert dominance in this way then you will have my hearty congratulations. I am nothing if not egalitarian and venomous.

—Gax, forcefully

DEAR GAX: I have two children, girls, aged 9 and 7. The 7-year-old shows all signs of becoming a great Gawxor warrior: she files her teeth on stones; she runs barefoot across the top of our wrought-iron fence; she's even taken to chitin-crusting her hair without being told (she keeps an ant farm in her room). The 9-year-old, however, never showed any interest at all—right now she's keen on becoming a veterinarian, although as you know, kids go through phases. Should I hold out hope? It is possible she may yet take up with the Ganzzax scribe tribe? Or should we accelerate the Gawxor indoctrination to make up for lost time?

—WANTS TWO GAWXORI

Dear Wants,

You white people trying to be Gaxian make me sick. You can't just read Wikipedia and watch a few movies and think you know what it's like to be Gaxian. Did you watch the burning moon of Gax'an collide with Gax-Prime? Did you dance with glee from webbed foot to webbed foot, anticipating the triennial Measuring of the Neck? Did you savor the taste of your first egg, knowing that each bite was eliminating heirs from your house? If you haven't, I recommend the very good book *Ganaxorr: A Handbook of Gaxian Ritual* by Professor Reed Barnes at NYU. *The Lonely Planet Guide to Gax* has some good stuff too. I am extensively quoted in both books, occasionally contradictingly.

Let your older daughter become a veterinarian. When your youngest goes through the Change it may be handy to have a relative with access to equine-strength drugs (depending on the status of the laws by then). This is what we call *gaxnat*, "living in concert." If any member of your family—or anyone reading—requires personal individualized consultation for any Ganaxorr, I am available on an hourly basis and will also consider working in exchange for waste varnish from any deck-refinishing projects you may be undertaking. That stuff is very tightly controlled where I come from.

—Gax, anticipatingly

DEAR GAX: I have a two-year-old son who is basically trouble incarnate. This child positively delights in doing things he knows he shouldn't, and thinks up new ways to aggravate me on a daily basis. His elder brother was a much easier child, so I'm at a loss for how to deal with the little weasel. He isn't old enough for time-outs yet. Any suggestions?

—EXHAUSTED PARENT

Dear Exhausted,

How have you been disciplining the child up till now? You say he is not old enough for time-outs, because he may not be developed enough to understand that ten minutes in a corner is supposed to be a punishment, rather than simply a considerate rest period before the next mischief. Yet even without a capacity for higher reasoning, the child, like any animal, will respond to more primitive stimulus.

Perhaps a more severe variant—a Super Time-Out, if you will—should be considered, where instead of being confronted with an abstract *absence* of stimulation (difficult to make the cognitive leap into behavior deterrence), the child is instead thrust into a stressful survival situation. For instance, if he teases the cat, submerge him immediately in a box of spiders. He will quickly learn not to tease the cat.

—*Gax, savagely*

DEAR GAX: I have trouble sleeping at night. Try as I might, my mattress seems entirely incapable of rendering any sort of comfort. Yet, I am stuck with the blasted thing: I cannot afford another mattress. What do you suggest I do to help myself sleep at night?

—*INVOLUNTARY INSOMNIAC*

Dear Involuntary,

If the mattress is the problem, then change it. Flip it around, turn it backwards, or place shirts or towels underneath your sheet to make it even more lumpy. Build it up into a nest rather than allowing it to be some flat thing that nobody likes. There is no prize for keeping your mattress unmolested until you die. Put things on it that are in the negative shape of your body, so you are cradled by these things. I cannot believe how many humans do not understand the importance of sleeping in a cradle position. Did your kinsmen never bend you over stones until you wept with comfort?

But this assumes the mattress is indeed the problem. Perhaps you are retiring with tension, your body unable to disengage from the worries of your day. You do not say whether you have stairs in your warren, but if you do, you should run up and down them twenty times before retiring. If you do not have stairs, you may run in place, but be sure your knees crest your navel. At each step say a nonsense syllable such as "dorp." Change the syllable each circuit. This will flush out your brain, soften your muscles, and make you deliciously limp so that ~~you will be unable to prevent yourself from being devoured~~ sleep will beg you to enter it.

As a last resort, hold an egg in your mouth as you go to bed. This will keep your thoughts occupied.

—*Gax, practically*

DEAR GAX: I want to lose weight, but never go to the gym. I want to become a writer, but lack the discipline to write on a daily basis. My car is in disrepair, my house is a mess. I seem to be suffering from chronic laziness. How can I whip myself into a more industrious lifestyle?

—*LAZY BONES*

Dear Lazy,

For what reason do you seek a life of furious industry? Being from a race that gathers into a hive formation each autumn, take it from me—there is no great benefit to working hard. Being even halfway competent at anything means you just end up crowded against a thousand other hand-picked Champions, trying to lift a billion-ton mountain and throw it into the sea, as has been prophesied by the Elders. But no matter how hard you strain and try to lift that mountain, it remains rooted in the soil as firmly as ever. I don't even know whose dumb idea it is to keep trying every year. *It doesn't even have handholds, you guys. That* would be a good place to start, and if the Council would still take my calls I would tell them so myself. I do not know if they read this column—due to their advanced age, their eyes may have tuned out of the visible-light phase by now.

What do you claim your problems are? According to your letter, you are fat and creatively dissatisfied, with a diseased car and a horrible house. Rivers have carved this deep canyon in you over time, and it is not so simple as saying "Go back uphill, river." This is your river on purpose, and the best you can do is dig a canal or make this downward-flowing river turn a turbine for your benefit. Recast your failings as strengths and attempt to view life with these "undesirable characteristics" as an immutable constant. What new opportunities present themselves that you may have overlooked? Can you be a fetish model for hoarders, or hire yourself out as a "before" specimen for infomercials? These are just a few examples. If you forget your petty ambitions and instead accept yourself as your life has thus far molded you, then technically this counts as a win for me and I get a bonus for this column without you even having to do anything.

—Gax, tolerantly

Gax is an alien from the planet Gax. He enjoys fishing, romance novels, and homicide. "Ask Gax" questions were submitted by readers at wondermark.com.

DEAR GAX: A close companion of mine is a Gaxian, and has given out invitations to, from what I could gather, is his wedding. What is the appropriate behaviour for a Gaxian wedding? Should I bring a gift? Wear any particular clothes? I'd hate to cause offense…

—NUPTIALS? NO CLUE

Dear Nuptials,

Consider yourself honored to have been invited to your first *gaxitan!* The *gaxitan* life-bonding ritual is an elaborate affair, steeped in tradition and often involving the participation of close family and friends. While the full *gaxitan* is unfortunately difficult to perform here on Earth, as ammonium nitrate can react explosively with your atmosphere, an abbreviated and modified form of the ceremony is often performed by expatriate Gaxians. Of course, depending on the faith and preferences of the six to eleven others being bonded to the prime *gaxitanta*, human traditions may be incorporated as well. A common one is stomping on a glass! Usually this comes after the *gaxitanta* has regurgitated the officiant.

It is not required to bring a gift, although again this may be perfectly fine in a blended ceremony. You should be careful to wear waterproof garb and shoes you do not mind burning. (You'll probably not want to take them home after the bonding, anyhow.) It's perfectly okay to wear some old grubbies, just enough so you can make it over the obsidian shards and find your seat. After the bonding, which will take place at the midpoint (around the ninth hour), you can leave your shoes off if the sticky ink fluid makes them uncomfortable. (Once the *gaxitanta* molts her carapace, you'll be able to make it back out over the shards just fine.) Just take some Dramamine beforehand, bring a scouring pad or old toothbrush, and most of all, have fun!

—Gax, joyfully

A Comprehensive Index Of

LAST LINES.

AUTHOR'S FAREWELL.

THANK YOU FOR READING my book! I enjoyed making it. Each of these books—this is now my fifth collection of Wondermark comics—is a unique design challenge for me; an attempt to create a presentational experience that's as compelling as the content it's presenting. I also enjoy having a reason to write in different voices, play around with different visual styles, and break a cardinal typographical rule by cramming as many fonts into one book as possible, *while still making it look good.*

HEARTY THANK-YOUS TO: Zachary Sigelko, Jeffrey Rowland, Holly Post, George Rohac, Kris Straub, Dave Kellett, Kevin McShane, my wife Nikki, and you. Yes, *you,* with your legs crossed and your head cocked slightly to one side. *You.* You're the best. Thank you.

C.A.S.U.A.L

G.A.X.I.A.N